THE PRECISION TRAP

CA ASIF MASANI

notionpress
.com

INDIA · SINGAPORE · MALAYSIA

ISBN
Paperback 979-8-90451-681-9
Hardcase 979-8-90540-344-6

Contents

Praise for the Precision Trap

"As finance professionals, all too often we focus on precision when speed is needed. Not because we are not trying to be fast, but because we want to be right and have every assumption buttoned up. Asif argues that we need to change the way we think. We cannot sacrifice speed for a little extra precision; in my experience, that little extra precision rarely changes the decision, but it often comes after the decision has been made. Asif clearly articulates this problem, provides lots of great examples through stories from practitioners and then provides practical frameworks for solving this problem. Highly recommend giving it a read."

Paul Barnhurst, Founder, The FP&A Guy | Podcast Host, FP&A Tomorrow and Financial Modeler's Corner

"I spent six months building a budget that a pandemic made obsolete overnight. That experience taught me something no finance qualification ever did. Precision in planning is worthless if the plan cannot survive contact with reality. The Precision Trap captures this truth and extends it far beyond budgeting. Asif Masani has written a book that every finance leader should read. Not because it tells you to cut corners, but because it forces you to ask the right question before you open Excel. The goal of finance is not to be right. It is to be useful. This book shows you the difference."

Ron Monteiro, Founder KICT Inc. | Keynote Speaker, Author and Trainer

"The Precision Trap names something the finance profession has needed named for a long time. Through my own work with finance teams across industries, I have seen the cost of analytical latency firsthand. Decisions made without finance, windows missed, insights delivered after the moment had passed. Asif Masani has articulated this pattern with precision and clarity, and more importantly, he has given finance professionals a practical framework for escaping it. This is not a book about doing finance differently. It is a book about understanding why finance must evolve and what to do about it."

Dr. Prashanth Southekal, PhD | Founder, DBP Institute | Author of Data for Business Performance, Analytics Best Practices and Data Quality.

Foreword

I have spent over two decades in finance leadership roles across multiple industries. I have built FP&A teams, sat in board rooms, advised CEOs on some of the most consequential decisions of their organizations' lives, and trained thousands of finance professionals on the technical craft of the function.

In all that time, nobody ever asked me the question that this book is built around.

Was the analysis fast enough to be useful?

Not accurate enough. Not thorough enough. Not defensible enough. **Fast enough to be useful.**

I first heard Asif Masani articulate this question in one of our early conversations about what was going wrong in finance teams we had both worked with and trained. We had both seen the same pattern from different angles. The exhaustive model that arrived after the decision. The fifty-slider deck that confirmed what the business had already committed to. The finance professional who was technically excellent and strategically invisible.

We had both felt the frustration of it. Neither of us had found the language for it.

Asif found the language. And then he wrote the book.

The Precision Trap is not a book about doing finance differently. It is a book about understanding why finance professionals do what they do. Why they were trained to optimise for accuracy above all else. Why that training made complete sense for the world that existed when it was designed. And why it has quietly become a liability in the world that finance teams are actually operating in today.

I have watched Asif build the FP&A Professionals Institute from the ground up. I have seen him teach these ideas to thousands of finance professionals across more than a hundred countries. I have seen the moment. It happens consistently, across every cohort, every geography, every level of seniority. When a finance professional hears the argument for the first time and recognises themselves in it.

That moment of recognition is what this book produces on every page.

I contributed two stories to this manuscript. Both are true. Both are uncomfortable. And both illustrate something that no textbook on financial analysis has ever captured. The cost of arriving too late is real, measurable, and almost entirely invisible to the finance teams responsible for it.

If you are a finance professional reading this, you will recognise yourself somewhere in these chapters. The question is not whether you have fallen into the precision trap. The question is whether you are willing to climb out.

Asif has written the map.

Dhawal Parvatikar CFO | Co-Founder, FP&A
Professionals Institute |
Director, CGFPA®

Acknowledgements

A book about the cost of arriving too late should, by its own logic, be written with the help of people who showed up early and stayed.

Several people did exactly that for this one.

Dhawal Parvatikar has been a thought partner, co-instructor, and collaborator throughout the building of FP&A Professionals Institute. He contributed two stories from the front lines of finance leadership to this manuscript and his fingerprints are on more of this work than a single acknowledgement can capture. The foreword he wrote for this book is the most honest endorsement I could have asked for.

Ron Monteiro gave me the story I did not know I needed. His honest account of a billion-dollar budget made obsolete overnight and the lesson it produced is one of the most vivid illustrations of the book's argument. I am grateful for his generosity and his candour.

Dr. Prashanth Southekal brought rigour and real numbers to a book that argues for both. The $3.2 million window, his story, his insight, his words, gives the argument a specificity that no composite case study could replicate. His line, delayed insights can be as costly as incorrect ones, belongs in the book because it belongs to him.

To the 150,000+ finance professionals who follow my work across LinkedIn and YouTube. This book began in your questions, your frustrations, and your quiet confessions that the business had already decided before the deck was ready. You are the reason this needed to be written.

To my parents, whose unwavering belief in me has been the foundation of everything I have built. To my wife **CA Kajal Masani**, for the patience, the space, and the belief that this was worth finishing.

And to every finance professional who has ever sat with the uncomfortable feeling that their best work arrived just a little too late. This book is for you. And you are capable of being earlier.

Asif Masani |
Co-Founder, FP&A Professionals Institute |
Director, CGFPA®

Disclaimer

The concepts and practices described in this book are broadly applicable to finance professionals across a wide range of roles and industries. While the book draws heavily on examples from Financial Planning and Analysis (FP&A), the argument it makes applies equally to Accountants, Auditors, CFOs, finance business partners, commercial finance leaders, controllers, and anyone whose work involves translating numbers into decisions.

Different organisations use different titles for similar finance functions. The patterns described in these pages are not specific to any one role, industry, or geography. They are specific to a culture that exists across all of them.

The stories in this book are drawn from two sources.

The first are real experiences shared by named contributors who have given explicit permission for their stories to be included and attributed.

The second are composite cases drawn from patterns observed across the finance community over many years of teaching, coaching, and working with finance professionals across more than a hundred countries. Composite stories are illustrative and do not represent any specific individual, organisation, or situation.

The author has made every effort to ensure the accuracy of the information contained in this book. Neither the author nor the publisher accepts responsibility for any errors or omissions.

The ideas and frameworks presented here are intended for professional development and reflection. They should be applied with judgement appropriate to the specific context, industry, and regulatory environment of the reader.

This book does not constitute financial, legal, or professional advice.

Introduction

Honestly, most of the time the business has already decided before our deck is ready.

The sentence was said quietly, during a coffee break.

The meeting had been running for three hours. The room was full of finance professionals, FP&A managers, business partnering leads, senior analysts from organizations across the industry. Their technical skills were not in question.

- Their financial models were sophisticated.
- Their variance analysis was airtight.
- Their presentations were clean and professionally structured.

During the break one of them said something that stopped me.

Honestly, most of the time the business has already decided before our deck is ready.

He was not complaining. He was not bitter. He said it the way people say things they have known for a long time and never quite found words for with a kind of quiet resignation that suggested this was simply the nature of things. Finance built the analysis. The business made the decision. The timing rarely aligned. That was just how it worked.

I drove home that evening thinking about that sentence.

Not because it was surprising. Because I had been hearing versions of it for years in consulting engagements, in CFO roundtables, in online communities, in the direct messages that finance professionals send when they are willing to say things publicly, they will not say in a room. The analysis was right. The team was capable. The decision had already moved.

I had been treating each instance as an isolated frustration. A communication problem. A resourcing problem. A technology problem. Something specific to that organization or that team or that leader.

That evening I understood it differently.

It was not a skill gap. It was not a process failure. It was not something that could be fixed with better software or a restructured team or a new business partnering framework.

It was a trap. Cultural, structural, and almost entirely invisible to the people inside it.

And someone needed to name it clearly.

Who is this Book For?

I picture you specifically.

You are a high-performing finance professional, an FP&A manager, a Finance Business Partner, a CFO who has been wondering why the function they lead is less influential than it should be. You are technically excellent. You have never been told your work is inaccurate or unprofessional or insufficient.

But something is off and you know it.

Recently perhaps last week, perhaps last month you spent significant time building a rigorous piece of analysis. A pricing model, an investment case, a commercial review. You built it carefully. You checked it thoroughly. You presented it well.

And in the meeting, or on the way home, or in the quiet moment after the debrief, you felt something you could not quite articulate.

Not anger. Not failure. Just a quiet sense of being slightly late to something important. A feeling that the room had already moved somewhere before you arrived. That the analysis confirmed a direction rather than shaped one. That your two weeks of careful work landed as validation rather than input.

That feeling has a name. This book is it.

You are good enough at your job to know something is wrong. Senior enough to see the pattern. And you are holding this book because some part of you suspects that fixing it requires something more fundamental than working harder or presenting better or asking your team to be more strategic.

You are right. It does.

WHAT THE TRAP ACTUALLY IS

The precision trap is not a character flaw. It is not laziness or incompetence or a lack of ambition.

It is an understandable, entirely career-rational response to an environment that has spent decades rewarding accuracy and never once measuring usefulness.

From the first day of an accounting qualification to the most recent performance review, finance professionals are evaluated on a single dimension. The number is right or it is wrong. The reconciliation ties or it does not. The analysis is thorough or it has gaps.

Nobody asks, did this analysis change a decision? Did it arrive in time to matter? Did the finance professional state a clear view or hide behind a range of scenarios?

Those questions are not asked because the answers are harder to measure than accuracy. And because the answers, if measured honestly, would reveal something uncomfortable about how finance functions in most organizations and about what the business has quietly stopped expecting from them.

The precision trap is the accumulated result of this measurement gap. Finance teams that have optimized, over years and decades, for the standard they are actually held to rather than the standard that would make them genuinely useful. Finance professionals who have built their professional identity around thoroughness and accuracy because those are the qualities that have always been rewarded and who have, without knowing it, sacrificed speed and judgement and influence in the process.

The trap is invisible from inside. That is what makes it a trap rather than a choice.

This book makes it visible.

WHAT THIS BOOK DOES

The Precision Trap is structured in three parts.

Part I names the trap. What it is, where it came from, what it costs, and why finance professionals cannot see it from inside. These five chapters are diagnostic. They are designed to produce the specific experience of recognition. The moment a reader thinks this is exactly what has been happening and I never had language for it before.

Part II gives the tools. Five specific, practical frameworks for escaping the trap.

- How to ask the right questions before starting any analysis.
- How to calibrate the accuracy dial to what the decision actually requires.
- How to build reusable analytical frameworks that get faster and smarter with every use.
- How to align with business partners before the work begins rather than after it is delivered.
- And how to communicate for action rather than for coverage.

These five chapters are immediately applicable. A finance professional who reads Part Two on a Sunday evening knows what to do differently on Monday morning.

PART THREE ADDRESSES THE HARDEST PART: THE CHANGE

- How to have the conversation with your CEO that renegotiates the implicit contract between finance and the business.
- How to shift your team's culture through the specific behaviours that matter under pressure rather than the announcements that do not.
- How to measure whether it is working.
- And what all of this means for the finance function as artificial intelligence removes the processing work that currently defines most of its time.

The book ends with a letter. Not a framework. A direct communication from one finance professional to another about what this work is really for and what becomes possible when the trap has been escaped.

The call came on a Thursday afternoon.

James Okafor had been CFO of a mid-sized manufacturing business for three years. He was, by any conventional measure, excellent at his job. The function he ran was tight, well-regarded, and consistently accurate. The board trusted his numbers. The CEO relied on his reporting. The management accounts closed on time every month without exception.

The call was from a headhunter. A private equity firm was looking for a CFO for one of their portfolio companies. Fast-growing. Commercially complex. The kind of role that required a finance leader who could operate at pace and influence decisions rather than document them.

The headhunter was direct.

We have looked at your profile. The technical credentials are exceptional. But we have spoken to a few people who know your work. The feedback we are getting is that your function is very strong on reporting and not yet strong on commercial influence.

Can you tell me about a decision your finance team shaped in the last six months?

James paused.

He thought about the last six months. The monthly accounts. The quarterly forecasts. The budget resubmission. The board pack that had taken his team three weeks to prepare and that the board had reviewed in forty minutes.

He thought about the decisions that had been made in that period. The new product launch. The pricing review. The supplier renegotiation. The market entry discussion that had eventually been shelved. He tried to identify one that his finance team had shaped. Not documented. Not validated after the fact.

Shaped means it arrived early enough, with a clear enough point of view, to change what the business decided.

He could not find one. He thanked the headhunter and said he would think about it. He did not call back. But he did not stop thinking about that question.

That evening he sat at his desk and looked at the function he had spent three years building. It was, by every standard he had ever been given, excellent. Accurate. Timely. Comprehensive. Professionally rigorous in every respect. And it had not shaped a single significant decision in six months.

Stephen Covey described a group of workers cutting their way through a jungle. They were moving fast. The tools were sharp. The process was efficient. Progress, by every available measure, was being made. Then someone climbed a tree, looked out over the canopy, and called down to the workers below.

Wrong jungle.

The workers were not incompetent. The tools were not blunt. The effort was not wasted in any technical sense. Every individual action was correct. The direction was wrong.

James Okafor had spent three years building an excellent finance function. His team could cut faster and more cleanly than almost any function he had seen. The tools were sharp. The process was disciplined. The output, by every available measure, was impressive.

He had simply never climbed the tree.

The question the headhunter had asked. Can you tell me about a decision your finance team shaped? was the view from the tree. And from up there, for the first time, James could see clearly what three years of excellent work had quietly failed to produce.

Not a reporting function. Not a validation function. Not a function that documented decisions after they were made with extraordinary accuracy and complete professional rigor.

A function that shaped decisions while they were still fluid. That was the jungle he had been trying to reach. He had just been cutting in the wrong direction.

THE PROMISE

If you read this book and apply what it contains, one thing changes above all others.

You stop being the person who validates decisions after they are formed. You become the person who shapes them while they are still fluid.

That shift from reactive to influential, from defensive to energizing, from slightly late to exactly on time does not require a new job title or a restructured team or a different organization. It requires a different orientation to the work you are already doing.

The analysis does not need to be less rigorous. It needs to be more useful.

The recommendation does not need to be less careful. It needs to arrive before the window closes.

The finance professional does not need to be less precise. They need to understand that precision in service of a decision that has already been made is not precision at all.

It is the most expensive answer in the room. This book is about learning to be earlier.

1

The Most Expensive Answer in the Room

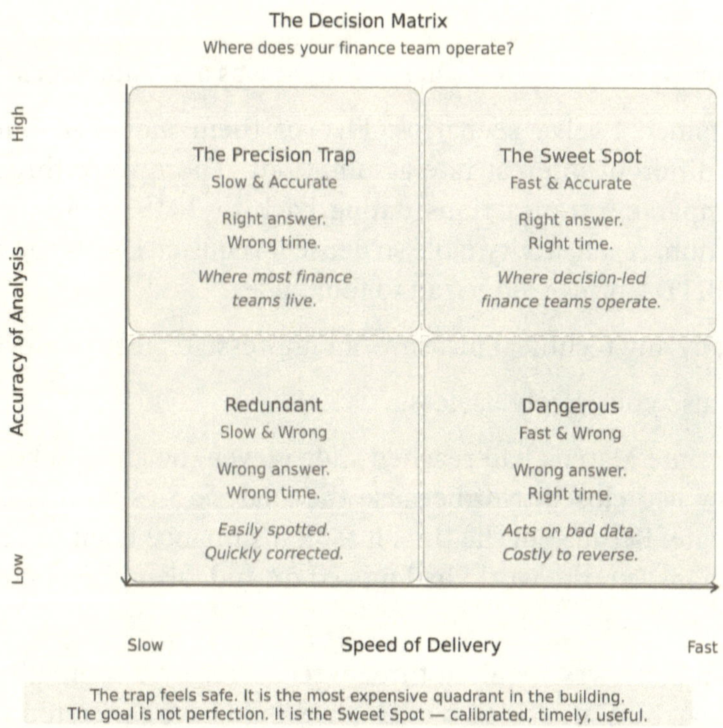

The email arrived at 11:47 pm on a Tuesday night.

Marcus Chen, the CEO of a mid-sized logistics company, had been waiting for it since Friday. His team had identified an acquisition target. It was a regional competitor that had quietly struggled through two bad years. And for the first time in its history, it was vulnerable. The window was narrow. The seller's banker had been clear: there were two other interested parties, a decision was expected by the end of week, and the price would not wait for the unprepared.

Marcus had asked his finance team for a preliminary view on Monday morning. Not a full valuation. Just enough to know whether the numbers made sense, whether the strategic fit was real. Whether to keep going or walk away.

A directional answer. A 70% answer, he had said. Something to work with.

What arrived at 11:47 on Tuesday night was a 47-slide deck.

It contained twelve scenarios. Five of them modelled outcomes under different interest rate assumptions. There were three pages on comparable transactions dating back to 2019. A Monte Carlo simulation. A sensitivity table so dense it required a separate legend. The EBITDA bridge alone ran to four slides.

It was, by any technical measure, an impressive piece of work.

It was also completely useless.

By the time Marcus had reached slide eleven, he already knew: the window had closed. Not because the analysis was wrong. Because it was late. Because in the time it took his finance team to build the perfect answer, the world had moved on and taken the opportunity with it.

The company was acquired three weeks later by a competitor. At a price that, by Marcus's own estimate, would have generated a return his board would have celebrated for years.

This book is about why that happens. And why it keeps happening. And what we can do about it.

The Time Value of Decisions

The value of an answer decays. Accuracy cannot reverse it.

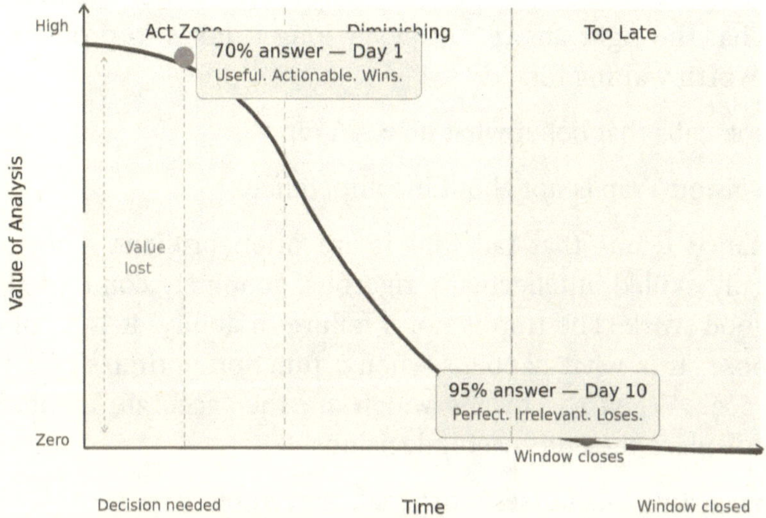

Like compound interest in reverse — delay doesn't just reduce value, it compounds the cost.
A 70% answer on Day 1 creates more value than a 100% answer on Day 10.

THE ILLUSION OF THE RIGHT ANSWER

There is a belief so deeply embedded in the culture of finance that most people who hold it have never once thought to question it. It feels less like an assumption and more like gravity. It is invisible, constant, and seemingly beyond debate.

The belief is this: the job of a finance team is to get the numbers right.

It sounds obviously true. It sounds like the very definition of the role. And in a narrow, technical sense, it is true. Accuracy matters. Errors are costly. And a finance function that consistently produces wrong numbers is not a finance function at all.

But there is a version of this belief that goes further, that quietly colonizes the culture of finance teams everywhere, and that turns a reasonable professional standard into something far more damaging.

It is the belief that precision that is exhaustive, comprehensive, leave-no-scenario-unmodelled precision is not just a standard but a virtue. That the more thorough the analysis, the better the finance team. That the right answer, however long it takes to produce, is always worth waiting for.

This book calls that belief what it is: A Trap.

The Precision Trap is not about incompetence.

The finance teams that fall into it are often brilliant. They are technically skilled, intellectually rigorous, genuinely committed to doing good work. The trap is not a failure of ability. It is a failure of purpose. It is what happens when a function optimizes for the wrong goal. When the means which are the "accurate numbers" quietly displace the end "useful decisions".

And it is costing businesses more than they know.

HOW WE GOT HERE...

To understand the Precision Trap, it helps to understand where the culture of finance comes from.

Modern corporate finance was built in an era of relative stability.

The analytical frameworks that still shape how finance teams work today. The discounted cash flow models, variance analysis, standard costing, annual budgets were largely developed in the mid-twentieth century. They were developed in an environment where industries moved slowly, competitive landscapes shifted over decades rather than quarters, and the cost of a wrong decision could be absorbed by the sheer momentum of large, stable organizations.

In that environment, precision made sense as the primary value.

If the world is not moving fast, the cost of taking three weeks to produce a thorough analysis is low. If decisions are largely reversible, the cost of being wrong is manageable. If your competitors are operating on the same slow clock, speed confers no particular advantage.

Finance training reflected this reality.

Accounting qualifications, MBA programs, CPA curriculum: all of them reward thoroughness, penalizes errors, and teach analytical rigor as the cardinal professional virtue. The message, delivered thousands of times across thousands of classrooms and examination halls, is consistent: get it right.

What those programs did not teach because the environment did not yet demand it. It was how to think about the tradeoff between accuracy and speed. How to decide, consciously and deliberately, **when a 70% answer delivered quickly is more valuable than a 95% answer delivered too late.** How to calibrate the depth of analysis to the urgency of the decision. How to be useful, not just correct.

The world those programs were training people for no longer exists.

The pace of business has changed beyond recognition. Competitive windows open and close in weeks. Acquisition opportunities evaporate. Market conditions shift mid-analysis. The cost of latency, which is the cost of waiting for the perfect answer, has risen sharply. While the culture and instincts of finance have remained largely unchanged.

The result is a profession optimized for a world that no longer exists, producing work that is technically excellent and strategically late.

THE ARGUMENT THIS BOOK MAKES

The central argument of The Precision Trap is simple, but its implications are radical.

The job of a finance team is not only to get the numbers right. The job is also to get the decisions right. And those are not the same thing.

A perfect analysis delivered after the decision has been made is not good finance.

It is an expensive way to be irrelevant. A directional analysis delivered in time to act with clear assumptions, honest uncertainty, and a point of view is what a business actually needs from its finance function.

Not someday, not ideally, but now, in the environment that businesses are actually operating in.

This is not an argument against rigor. It is an argument for relevance. The most rigorous thing a finance team can do is ask, before beginning any piece of analysis: what decision does this need to enable, and when does that decision need to be made?

Everything else, the depth of the model, the number of scenarios, the precision of the assumptions should flow from the answer to that question. Not from a professional habit. Not from anxiety about being wrong. Not from a culture that conflates thoroughness with quality.

The finance teams that businesses rely on most are the ones pulled into decisions early, not handed the outcome to model after the fact. They earn genuine trust. They are not the most accurate teams. They are the most useful ones.

They have, consciously or not, escaped the Precision Trap. This book is about how they did it, and how others can follow.

WHAT THE FOLLOWING CHAPTERS WILL SHOW

The chapters ahead build this argument in three parts.

The first part diagnoses the problem in full. We will look at where the Precision Trap comes from the training, the incentives, the cultural norms that make precision feel like virtue rather than choice. We will examine what it actually costs, in missed opportunities, delayed decisions, and the slow erosion of trust between finance and the businesses it serves. And we will meet the CEOs and operators who have felt the cost most acutely. People who stopped asking their finance teams certain questions not because they stopped needing answers, but because the answers always arrived too late.

The second part introduces a framework for escaping the trap. A set of principles and practices that the best finance teams already use, often intuitively, and that can be made explicit and teachable. This includes how to tier decisions by urgency and reversibility, how to set explicit the Accuracy Dial before beginning any analysis, how to build decision templates for the choices a business makes repeatedly, and how to have the conversation with business leaders that most finance teams never have: how fast do you need this, and how precise does it need to be?

The third part is about implementation. How to shift the culture of a finance team from one oriented around accuracy to one oriented around decision impact. This is the hardest part, and the book will not pretend otherwise. Changing a professional culture is slow, uncomfortable work. But the finance leaders who have done it describe the result in consistent terms: their teams became more trusted, more influential, and more engaged. Because they were finally doing work that changed outcomes, rather than work that documented them.

A Note on What This Book Is Not

Before we go further, one clarification is worth making.

The Precision Trap is not an argument for sloppiness. It is not a brief for cutting corners, abandoning rigor, or producing careless work. A finance team that consistently delivers wrong numbers is not a useful finance team. It is a dangerous one, and nothing in these pages should be read as encouragement to become one.

The argument is more precise than that, and more uncomfortable.

It is that the culture of finance has produced teams that are excellent at a thing that businesses need less than they think, and poor at a thing that businesses need more than they realise. **The goal is not to stop being rigorous. It is to be rigorous about the right things.** And to have the professional confidence to be deliberately imprecise about the rest.

That confidence, it turns out, is the hardest thing to build.

It requires finance professionals to act against their training, their instincts, and the performance standards by which they have always been measured. It requires them to say, out loud, to a business leader: **here is what we know, here is what we don't, and here is what we think you should do.** And knowing that they could have been more certain if they had taken three more weeks.

The finance teams that can say that sentence are the ones that get invited into the room early. The ones that cannot are the ones who receive the email at 11:47 on a Tuesday night, after the decision has already been made for them.

Marcus Chen's finance team received that email, three weeks later, from the acquiring company's press office.

They had been right about everything. They had just been right too late.

In the next chapter, we will look more closely at where the Precision Trap comes from and why it is so difficult to see from the inside.

2

The Making of a Precision Culture

Sarah had been in finance for six years when she received the best performance review of her career.

Her manager, a careful and well-respected VP of Finance, spent the first ten minutes of the meeting working through her contributions over the previous twelve months. The forecasting work was solid. The variance analysis was thorough. The business partnering was developing well.

Then he leaned forward slightly.

"I want to highlight something specific," he said. "The board presentation in Q3. You caught a rounding error in the revenue bridge that nobody else had spotted. It was a small number but it would have been embarrassing. That kind of attention to detail is exactly what this team stands for."

Sarah left the meeting feeling genuinely proud. She had been seen. She had been recognised for doing her job well.

What neither she nor her manager discussed. What neither of them thought to discuss was something else that had happened in Q3.

The board presentation had been delayed by eleven days while the model was refined and stress-tested and reviewed. The decision to accelerate expansion into a new market had been pushed back as a result. By the time the board approved the move, a competitor had announced their own entry into the same market.

The window of first-mover advantage, which the original business case had been built around, was gone.

The rounding error Sarah caught was worth approximately $5,000 in the context of a $40 million decision.

The eleven-day delay cost the company something that was never calculated, never attributed, and never discussed in any performance review.

This is how precision culture sustains itself. Not through ill will. Not through incompetence. Through the entirely reasonable act of rewarding the things that are visible and measurable, while the costs of what is invisible and diffuse accumulate quietly in the background.

BUILT FOR A DIFFERENT WORLD

To understand why finance culture is the way it is, you have to understand the world it was built for.

The analytical frameworks that still shape how finance teams operate today were largely developed in the middle of the twentieth century. Discounted cash flow analysis, standard costing, variance reporting, the annual budgeting cycle.

These tools were designed in an era when industries moved slowly, competitive landscapes shifted over decades rather than quarters, and large organizations had the momentum to absorb the cost of decisions made carefully rather than quickly.

In that world, precision was not just a professional virtue. It was the correct strategic priority. If your competitors are operating on the same slow clock, taking three weeks to produce a thorough analysis costs you nothing. If decisions are largely irreversible and the stakes of being wrong are high, the case for waiting until you are certain is strong.

If the business environment is stable enough that a model built in January is still largely accurate in December, then investing deeply in getting that model right makes complete sense.

The professional standards that govern finance were written in this context. The accounting qualifications established in the mid-twentieth century were designed to produce professionals who could be trusted to produce accurate, auditable, defensible numbers.

The performance management systems built around those qualifications measured output quality meaning correctness above almost everything else. The entire infrastructure of finance as a profession was optimized, quite rationally, for a world where accuracy was the scarcest and most valuable resource a finance team could offer.

That world no longer exists.

The pace of business has changed beyond recognition in the last thirty years. Decision cycles that once took quarters now take weeks. Competitive intelligence that was once proprietary is now largely symmetrical. Everyone has access to roughly the same market data, the same industry reports, the same publicly available financial information. The advantage in most markets no longer goes to the company with the most accurate analysis. It goes to the company that acts on good enough analysis faster than everyone else.

The cost of waiting for the perfect answer (latency) has risen sharply. The culture and instincts of finance have not kept pace. The result is a profession optimized for a world that has largely disappeared, producing work that is technically excellent and strategically late.

How the Pipeline Reproduces Itself

The Precision Trap Pipeline

How precision culture reproduces itself — at every stage of a finance career

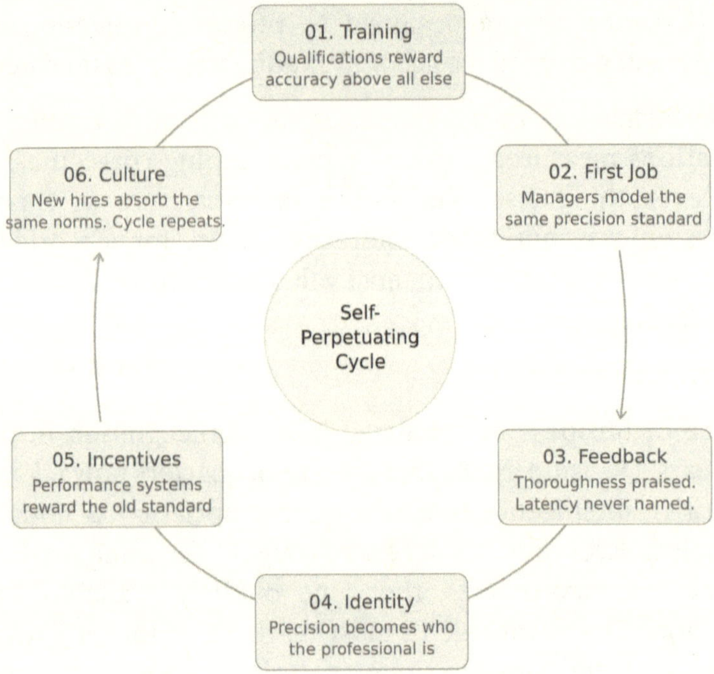

The cycle breaks only when metrics, language and feedback loops change simultaneously.

If precision culture were simply a historical accident, it would be easier to correct.

The more uncomfortable truth is that it actively reproduces itself at every stage of a finance professional's development. From their first accounting course to their most senior performance review.

Consider what finance education actually teaches. Professional accounting qualifications the CA, CPA, ACCA, CMA are built around a core premise: errors are unacceptable.

The examinations that produce qualified finance professionals test analytical accuracy with a rigor that few other professions match.

A misplaced decimal point fails a paper. A wrong assumption invalidates a conclusion. The message, delivered thousands of times across thousands of examination halls, is consistent and clear: in finance, getting it right is the only standard that matters.

This is not a criticism of those qualifications. Accuracy genuinely matters. A finance professional who consistently produces wrong numbers is not a useful finance professional. They are dangerous. The problem is not that accuracy is taught. The problem is that it is taught in isolation, as an absolute virtue rather than a contextual choice, without any accompanying discussion of the tradeoffs that precision requires.

Nobody in any professional finance qualification asks the question: **was this analysis fast enough to be useful?** The concept of analytical latency. The cost of taking too long does not appear in any curriculum. The tradeoff between accuracy and speed is never explicitly named, never debated, never given a framework. It simply does not exist as a topic in formal finance education.

The same pattern continues into the workplace. Graduate finance programs at major corporations are designed to produce technically excellent analysts.

Mentors and managers themselves are products of the same precision culture. They pass on the same instincts. The performance management systems that evaluate finance teams reward output quality, measured almost entirely as accuracy, and rarely if ever measure decision impact whether the analysis arrived in time to change anything.

At every stage, the feedback loops point in the same direction. Be accurate. Be thorough. Be defensible. The finance professional who delivers a precise answer three weeks late receives a better performance review than the one who delivers a directional answer in two days. Not because their manager is wrong, but because the system they are both operating in has no mechanism for valuing speed.

The pipeline does not produce professionals with a blind spot. It produces professionals who were never shown that there was anything to see.

Richard had done everything right.

He had attended the leadership program. He had read the books on strategic finance. He had restructured his team around business partnering rather than functional silos. He had hired a finance business partnering specialist from a company renowned for its commercial finance capability. He had run a team offsite where everyone agreed, genuinely and enthusiastically, that the function needed to evolve from a reporting team into a decision support team.

That was eighteen months ago.

On a Tuesday morning in October, he sat in a leadership meeting and watched something that had become, without his fully noticing, entirely familiar. His senior analyst was presenting the quarterly commercial review. She was on slide eight. She was still explaining the methodology.

The CFO of the operating division, a direct, commercially sharp leader, was looking at his phone. Richard knew what was coming. Three more slides of methodology. Two slides of charts. And then, on slide thirteen, the actual insight the room had been waiting for since the meeting began.

After the meeting the divisional CFO stopped Richard in the corridor.

I don't know what to do with your team, he said. Not unkindly. They work incredibly hard. The analysis is always right. But by the time it arrives I have already made the call. I am not sure what I am supposed to do with it after the fact.

Richard went back to his desk and sat for a long time. He had changed the structure. He had changed the language. He had hired differently, trained deliberately, and communicated the vision with complete sincerity. He had done everything the transformation playbooks recommended. And the culture had absorbed every single one of those changes without materially shifting.

The team was still building for comprehensiveness. Still presenting methodology before insight. Still arriving after the decision rather than before it. Still, in every way that actually mattered to the business, operating exactly as it had before the transformation began.

Richard did not yet have the language for what he was experiencing. But Dr. Jason Fung, writing about a completely different kind of problem, had described it with uncomfortable precision.

Fung's work on obesity identified something that decades of conventional dietary advice had missed entirely.

The reason diets fail, he argued, is not willpower. It is the body's internal thermostat, what he called the body set weight. Everybody has a set point that it defends with extraordinary persistence. Cut calories and the body fights back. Metabolism slows. Hunger hormones rise. The thermostat, sensing that the temperature has dropped below its setting, turns the heat back up.

The dieter experiences this as personal failure. It is actually biology working exactly as designed.

The only way to change the outcome permanently is not to fight the thermostat. It is to reset it. To change the internal calibration so that the body defends a different set point. Not through more willpower applied to the existing setting. Through a fundamentally different intervention that changes the setting itself.

Richard's finance team had a thermostat. It was set to comprehensiveness, to defensibility, to methodology before insight. And very intervention he had tried: the restructure, the new hire, the offsite, the vision statement: had been the organizational equivalent of cutting calories. Temporarily effective. Ultimately absorbed. The thermostat had turned the heat back up every time.

What Richard needed was not another initiative. He needed to reset the thermostat.

The question was how?

THE ART OF STAYING INVISIBLE

There is a reason the precision trap is so difficult to recognise from the inside.

It is not simply that finance professionals are too busy or too comfortable to examine their own assumptions. It is that the trap is structurally designed to conceal itself.

The first layer of concealment is that the work looks right. A finance team deep in the precision trap is not producing bad work by any conventional measure. The models are well-built. The assumptions are documented. The scenarios are stress-tested. When the analysis finally arrives late, comprehensive, technically impeccable. There is nothing in the document itself that reveals the cost of its latency. It looks like excellent finance work because, by the standards finance teams have been given, it is.

The second layer of concealment is that the cost of being late is almost never attributed correctly. When a decision goes badly because the analysis arrived too slowly, the post-mortem rarely identifies the finance team as a contributing factor. The competitor moved faster. The market shifted. The timing was unfortunate. These are the explanations that get written into board papers and lessons-learned documents. The causal link between analytical latency and decision quality is diffuse, hard to prove, and uncomfortable to raise. So, it goes unraveled.

This is what behavioural economists call an attribution error.

The systematic misidentification of causes when the feedback is delayed and indirect. The finance team that spent three weeks perfecting a model never sees the cost of those three weeks. They see the quality of the model. They receive praise for its thoroughness. The cost lands elsewhere in the organization, attributed to other causes, absorbed by people who may not even know that a faster answer could have changed the outcome.

THE THIRD LAYER OF CONCEALMENT IS PSYCHOLOGICAL.

Daniel Kahneman's work on thinking identified two modes of cognition. Fast, intuitive thinking and slow, deliberate thinking. Slow thinking feels more trustworthy. It feels more responsible. It feels more professional. Finance culture is essentially a profession-wide institutionalization of the preference for slow thinking, applied uniformly regardless of whether the situation actually calls for it.

A finance professional who delivers a rough answer quickly is taking a professional risk. If the rough answer turns out to be wrong, they are exposed. A finance professional who delivers a precise answer slowly is protected. If the answer arrives too late, the cost lands elsewhere.

If the answer turns out to be right, they receive credit for thoroughness. The incentive structure, seen clearly, actively rewards latency and penalizes speed.

Not intentionally. But effectively.

WHY THE COST IS HIGHER NOW THAN EVER

Precision culture has always had costs.

But three specific changes in the business environment have made those costs significantly higher than they were when the culture was formed.

THE FIRST IS THE COMPRESSION OF DECISION CYCLES.

Research on corporate decision-making consistently shows that the time available to make significant strategic decisions has shortened dramatically over the last three decades. What once took a quarter now takes weeks. What once took weeks now takes days. The window between a decision becoming available and that decision becoming irreversible has narrowed in almost every industry. A finance team operating on a three-week analytical cycle in an environment where decisions need to be made in one week is not just slow, it is structurally incapable of being useful.

THE SECOND IS THE DEMOCRATIZATION OF DATA

In the era when precision culture formed, proprietary data was a genuine competitive advantage. Companies that had better information than their competitors could afford to analyse it slowly because the information itself was the edge. That advantage has largely disappeared. The data available to one competitor is broadly available to all. In this environment, the edge goes not to the company with the most accurate analysis but to the company that acts on good enough analysis fastest. Precision, in a world of symmetrical information, is a diminishing return.

THE THIRD IS THE CHANGING NATURE OF DECISIONS THEMSELVES.

A growing proportion of significant business decisions are reversible in ways they were not a generation ago. Digital products can be modified after launch. Market entries can be tested before full commitment. Pricing can be adjusted in real time. The classic argument for precision that the cost of being wrong is too high to risk is simply less true for a large and growing category of decisions. A finance culture that treats every decision as irreversible, and demands the certainty appropriate for irreversible decisions before advising on any of them, is misapplying its own standards.

The precision trap was always a trap. It is now a more expensive one than it has ever been.

THE INVISIBLE CURRICULUM

Sarah, the finance professional from the opening of this chapter, is not unusual. She is, in almost every respect, exactly what the finance profession set out to produce. Accurate. Thorough. Attentive to detail. Trusted by her manager and her peers.

What she was never taught. What the system that trained her had no mechanism for teaching was **how to think about the tradeoff between accuracy and speed.**

How to ask, before beginning any piece of analysis: what decision does this need to enable, and when does that decision need to be made?

How to calibrate the depth of her work to the urgency of the question rather than to the professional standard of thoroughness she had been trained to meet regardless of context.

That missing lesson absent from every qualification, every training program, every performance review she had ever received is what this book calls the invisible curriculum.

It is the set of things finance professionals need to know that their profession has never thought to teach them.

The chapters ahead are an attempt to write that curriculum down.

But first, we need to understand the full weight of what the precision trap costs. Not in the abstract. In the specific, measurable, sometimes devastating terms of real decisions made by real companies where the answer arrived just a little too late.

That is where we turn next.

3

What it Actually Costs

There is a number that never appears in any financial report. It does not show up in the variance analysis. It is not captured in the post-mortem. It does not get discussed in the board meeting, or the management review, or the lessons-learned document that gets filed and forgotten. It has no line item, no owner, and no accountability structure.

It is the cost of the answer that arrived too late.

Every organization carries this number. Most have no idea how large it is. And the reason they have no idea is not negligence or oversight. It is something more structural and more troubling. The cost of analytical latency is, by its nature, invisible. It lands in the wrong place, gets attributed to the wrong cause, and disappears into the noise of normal business life.

This chapter makes it visible.

What follows are seven stories. They come from different industries, different sizes of organization, different types of decisions. But they share a single common thread. A moment where the analysis was right, the team was capable, and the outcome was worse than it needed to be because the answer arrived just a little too late.

The numbers in these stories are real in the sense that matters.

Not in the sense that they happened to a specific named company on a specific named date but in the sense that they happen, in almost identical form, to companies everywhere, every week, without anyone ever writing them down.

STORY ONE: THE WINDOW THAT CLOSED ON A WEDNESDAY

You have already met this story. It opened Chapter One: the CFO, the acquisition, the 51-slide deck that arrived three and a half days after the window had closed. That was Story One. What follows are six more, each from a different industry, each with a different cost.

STORY TWO: THE PRICE THAT SHOULD HAVE BEEN HIGHER

The head of commercial finance at a fast-growing technology services company had a problem he recognised but could not solve.

Every six months, as the company's annual contract renewal cycle approached, the sales leadership team would ask the same question: where should we set pricing for the next period? The market had moved. Competitors had repriced. Customer willingness to pay had shifted. The answer required synthesizing customer data, competitive intelligence, margin analysis, and demand modelling.

And every six months, the answer came back in roughly the same form. A detailed pricing model, built from scratch, taking three to four weeks, arriving approximately ten days before the renewal conversations were scheduled to begin.

Ten days was, theoretically, enough time. In practice it was not.

By the time the analysis arrived, the sales team had already been having informal conversations with customers for weeks. They had already anchored the renewal discussions around price points they had developed from instinct and experience. They had already, in many cases, made implicit commitments about what the renewal would look like.

The finance team's analysis, careful, thorough, well-evidenced consistently showed that the company was underpricing its core product by between 8% and 12%. The data was clear.

Customer retention was high. Net promoter scores were strong. Switching costs were significant. The market would bear a higher price.

But the sales team, already mid-conversation with customers, could not act on this finding. Moving pricing by 8% to 12% after informal anchor conversations had been set would damage relationships and create internal conflict. The analysis arrived too late to change behaviour.

This happened six times across three years.

In year four, the commercial finance head did something different. He built a pricing template, a pre-structured model that could be updated with current data in approximately four hours, rather than rebuilt from scratch over four weeks. He ran the analysis eight weeks before renewal conversations began, not two weeks before. He presented it in a single page: headline recommendation, three supporting data points, confidence level, and what would need to change to move the number.

Sales got the answer early enough to anchor their conversations differently.

That renewal cycle, average contract value increased by 9.3%.

The difference between the old approach and the new one was not the quality of the analysis. The model was almost identical. The difference was when the answer arrived. And the form in which it was delivered. The same finance professional, the same data, the same underlying insight. Six times too late. Once in time.

The cumulative underpricing across those three years, calculated retrospectively, ran to several million dollars in forgone revenue. None of it appeared in any variance report. It was simply revenue that was never earned, from contracts that were never priced correctly, because the answer that could have changed the conversation arrived after the conversation had already been shaped.

STORY THREE: THE QUESTIONS THAT STOPPED BEING ASKED

James had been the CEO of a professional services firm for eleven years when he made a decision that, looking back, marked the moment his relationship with his finance team fundamentally changed.

The firm was considering opening an office in a new geography. Not a major expansion, just a satellite presence, three or four people, testing whether a market was real before committing more substantially. The kind of decision that, in James's experience, needed a few pieces of information: rough cost of establishment, estimated time to breakeven, and a sense of the revenue opportunity.

He asked his CFO for a view.

What came back, two weeks later, was a 34-page business case. It included a five-year P&L projection for the new office, a risk register with eleven identified risks and corresponding mitigation strategies, a sensitivity analysis across four key assumptions, a benchmarking exercise comparing the firm's proposed approach against six competitors who had entered the same market, and a recommendation section that concluded. After all the thirty-four pages it concluded that further research was needed before a decision could be made.

James read the document carefully. It was excellent work. It was also the answer to a question he had not asked.

He had asked: does this make rough sense, and should we take the next step?

He had received: here is everything we could possibly know about this decision, and we still cannot tell you what to do.

He approved the office opening anyway, based on his own judgment and a conversation with two partners who knew the market. The decision turned out to be correct. The office became profitable in its third year.

But something shifted after that document arrived.

In the years that followed, James stopped asking his finance team certain questions. Not formally, not consciously but the pattern was unmistakable. When he was considering a new service line, he called a trusted partner. When he was thinking about an acquisition, he rang an advisor. When he needed a quick read on whether a commercial arrangement made sense, he did the back-of-envelope calculation himself.

He did not stop trusting his finance team. He stopped expecting them to be useful for the kind of questions that mattered most to him. The fast, directional, uncertain questions that real business leadership generates constantly. He had learned, through experience, that asking those questions of his finance team produced documents rather than answers. So, he stopped asking.

The CFO, who was genuinely talented and deeply committed to the firm, never knew this had happened. From where she sat, the relationship with the CEO was strong. She was invited to board meetings. She was consulted on major decisions. She produced excellent, comprehensive, accurate work.

What she did not know was that the most important commercial decisions in the firm were being made in conversations she was not part of. And not because she was excluded, but because her CEO had quietly learned that including her created delay without adding proportionate value.

The cost of this dynamic is almost impossible to calculate. Some of those decisions would have been better with finance involved. Some of the risks James took on instinct would have looked different with a financial lens applied early. The opportunities that finance could have spotted and didn't, because they were never asked are unknowable.

What is knowable is this: in eleven years of leading a professional services firm, the CEO had gradually and completely rerouted his decision-making away from the function whose explicit purpose was to support it. Not because the function was bad. Because it had trained him, through repeated experience, that asking questions of finance produced thoroughness when he needed speed.

STORY FOUR: THE SHADOW TEAM

In a large retail organization, something had been quietly growing for three years before anyone in the finance function noticed it.

The head of digital commerce. A fast-moving, analytically capable leader who had joined from a technology company had built a team.

Not officially. There was no org chart entry, no budget line, no job descriptions reviewed by HR. But over three years, she had hired four people into roles with titles like "commercial analyst," "growth insights manager," and "digital performance lead." Their actual function, understood by everyone who worked with them, was to answer the questions that finance couldn't answer fast enough.

When the digital team needed to know whether a promotional mechanic was working, they ran their own analysis. When they needed to model the impact of a pricing change, they built their own model. When they needed to understand customer acquisition economics in a new channel, they did it themselves.

The finance team, two floors away, was producing excellent work. Monthly management accounts, closed on time. Quarterly forecasts, well-constructed and thoroughly reviewed. Annual budgets, comprehensive and defensible.

What the finance team was not producing was answers in the time frame that a digital commerce function actually operates in. Digital commerce moves in days and sometimes hours. A promotional campaign has a 72-hour window. A channel investment decision needs a view by the end of week. A pricing test needs to be evaluated before the test period ends.

Finance, operating on its normal cycle, could not serve this. So, the digital team built its own finance capability and stopped asking.

The cost of this arrangement was visible in three places once someone looked.

The first was direct cost. Four people performing work that was already being performed by the finance function, paid for twice by the same organization.

The second was consistency. The digital team's models used different assumptions, different data sources, and different methodologies than the finance team's models. When the two teams presented conflicting numbers to the same leadership meeting which happened, with increasing awkwardness, several times a year. It undermined the credibility of both.

The third was strategic. The digital function, operating with its own analytical capability, had gradually become functionally independent of the finance oversight that should have been shaping its investment decisions. Decisions were being made and implemented before finance had any visibility. By the time the numbers showed up in the management accounts, the commitments had already been made.

The CFO who eventually inherited this situation described it in a single sentence: ***"The business had stopped waiting for us. So, they stopped needing us. And once they stopped needing us, we lost the ability to influence anything that actually mattered."***

The shadow team was eventually dissolved and the four roles were integrated into a newly structured finance business partnering model. But the trust, once lost, took years to rebuild. And the decisions made during those three years without adequate financial oversight included several that, with better analysis applied earlier, would have looked very different.

STORY FIVE: THE BUDGET THAT 2020 MADE OBSOLETE

In the spring of 2020, a Senior Finance Director at a billion-dollar consumer packaged goods company was doing what his team did every year.

The annual budget process had kicked off the previous June. It ran until November. It involved stakeholders from across the organization, including manufacturing, commercial, supply chain and finance, each completing detailed input models that took hours, sometimes days to build.

The collective effort was enormous. Thousands of hours went into constructing what the organization hoped would be a precise view of the coming year.

This particular company manufactured toilet paper, paper towels, and facial tissue.

The budget was completed on schedule. It was thorough, well-constructed, and defensible across every assumption. January and February of 2021 were normal months. Actual results tracked closely against the plan.

Then March 2020 arrived. The pandemic hit.

Demand for the company's products did not just increase. It exploded.

From a budgeting perspective, the plan that had taken six months and thousands of collective hours to build was instantly obsolete. Not partially wrong. Not in need of revision. Completely irrelevant to the business reality the company was now operating in.

They had to throw it out. Entirely.

What followed was a forced experiment in a different kind of planning. Instead of an annual budget built for precision, the finance team shifted to high-level sprint forecasts which was shorter, more flexible, updated frequently.

These forecasts did not attempt to model every variable to two decimal places. They attempted to answer one question: **What does the business need to know right now to make the next decision?**

The sprint forecasts were directional. They were imprecise by the standards of the annual budget process. And they were, by every measure that actually mattered, far more useful.

The experience produced a reframe that stayed with the finance director long after the pandemic had passed. Perhaps the goal should not be to build the most precise budget possible.

Perhaps the goal should be to build a useful budget quickly at a level of detail that actually supports decision-making. Because in the end, the goal of budgeting is not precision. It is preparation.

STORY SIX: THE $3.2 MILLION WINDOW

An FP&A team at a mid-sized logistics firm in the United States was asked a question their leadership needed answered urgently: **what would happen to demand if prices were increased by one percent?**

The company was experiencing rising operational costs on fuel, warehousing and logistics overheads. A modest price increase would protect margins. But leadership needed confidence in the demand impact before moving. The analysis, on the surface, was straightforward.

In reality it was not. The data required to model price elasticity was scattered across multiple systems: ERP platforms, pricing tools, demand planning databases. There were no pre-built elasticity models. The team had to manually extract, clean, and reconcile the data before any analysis could begin. Frequent back-and-forth with data engineering teams slowed progress further.

The insight generation process was delayed by three to four weeks.

During those weeks, the business chose not to implement the price increase. Without clarity on the demand impact, leadership were not willing to move. And while they waited, market conditions shifted. Competitors began adjusting their prices dynamically.

The firm experienced a temporary surge in demand driven by seasonal factors, a window of high-volume, price-inelastic purchasing that would not last.

When the FP&A team finally completed the analysis, the results were clear. The majority of the firm's SKUs exhibited inelastic demand.

A one percent price increase would have produced only a marginal decline in volume approximately 0.2 to 0.3 percent resulting in a net positive impact on revenue.

The analysis was right. It arrived after the window had closed.

The company had kept its prices unchanged through a period of peak demand when a modest increase would have been absorbed with minimal volume loss. The estimated cost of that delay: $3.2 million in potential incremental revenue that was never earned.

Beyond the financial impact, something else shifted. Leadership's confidence in the FP&A team's ability to deliver timely insights and to be useful when it mattered had been quietly damaged. Not through any dramatic confrontation.

Through the accumulated experience of asking finance a question and receiving the answer after the moment had passed. As the finance director who lived through this experience later reflected: **in fast-moving markets, delayed insights can be as costly as incorrect ones.**

STORY SEVEN: THE INVOICE THAT NEVER CAME

The CFO of a mid-sized advertising agency had a working capital problem that nobody had named properly.

His company managed large-scale influencer and digital marketing campaigns for clients. Each project involved eight to ten influencers across different channels: social media, video, search each generating their own performance data: impressions, follower growth, lead counts, click-through rates. Before the agency could bill the client, it needed invoices and supporting documentation from every influencer and third party involved.

The documentation, in practice, trickled in slowly. Influencers submitted invoices on their own timelines. Supporting data arrived in different formats from different platforms. The finance team, trained to bill only when the complete picture was available, waited.

They gathered. They chased. They reconciled. And they waited for the last invoice.

The result was a billing cycle that took forty to forty-five days from project completion just to collect sufficient documentation before a single invoice had been raised to the client. The client then took thirty to thirty-five days to pay. From the date of service delivery to the date of cash receipt: ninety days. Sometimes more.

The agency was, in effect, financing its clients and its influencer partners simultaneously, paying vendors from its own cash while waiting for documentation that was holding up billing that was holding up payment.

The CFO identified the mechanism clearly. His finance team was optimizing for complete billing and waiting until every supporting document was in hand before raising any invoice. It was the correct instinct for a function trained to bill accurately. It was the wrong instinct for a business with vendors to pay and a working capital cycle that was slowly strangling it.

The fix was not more rigorous documentation chasing. It was a different philosophy about when good enough was enough.

He broke the billing process into stages. The moment a first invoice arrived with its supporting documentation even if eight others were still outstanding. The team billed for that portion. Partial billing against the project PO was permissible under the client contract. It had simply never been used, because the finance team had never considered billing anything less than the complete picture.

The result surprised even him. Sixty to seventy percent of each project's value was billable within the first two weeks of documentation arriving.

By billing progressively rather than waiting for completion, the agency began receiving sixty to seventy percent of its project cash within thirty to forty-five days of service delivery, rather than ninety days plus for the whole amount.

The last twenty-five to thirty percent of documentation the invoices that trickled in late, the supporting data that required chasing still arrived slowly. But its arrival no longer held up the majority of the cash the business was owed.

The finance team had been waiting for the perfect invoice. What the business needed was the useful solution.

THE PATTERN BENEATH THE STORIES

Seven stories. Seven industries. Seven different types of cost.

1. A consumer goods company that lost a transformational acquisition because a 51-slide deck took three and a half days to build, told in full in Chapter One.
2. A technology services company that underpriced its core product for three years because the analysis always arrived after the commercial conversations had already been shaped.
3. A professional services firm whose CEO gradually stopped asking his finance team the questions that mattered most, not in anger, but in quiet resignation.
4. A retailer whose most dynamic business unit built its own finance function rather than wait for the real one.
5. A billion-dollar consumer goods company whose finance team spent six months building a precise annual budget that a single month made entirely obsolete, and discovered, in the wreckage, that sprint forecasts served the business better than perfection ever had.
6. A logistics company that left $3.2 million in incremental revenue on the table because a price elasticity analysis arrived three weeks after the window of peak demand had already closed.
7. An advertising agency whose finance team waited forty-five days to raise a single invoice, financing both clients and vendors, because it would not bill until the last document arrived.

In none of these stories did the finance team do bad work. In all of them, the work was technically sound, professionally rigorous, and produced by capable people who genuinely cared about getting it right.

That is what makes the precision trap so difficult to address. The problem is not incompetence. It is not laziness. It is not a lack of effort or intelligence or commitment.

It is a systematic mismatch between what finance teams are optimised to produce and what the businesses they serve actually need.

And the cost of that mismatch, the missed acquisition, the forgone revenue, accumulates silently, attributed to other causes, invisible in every report and every review, until the moment someone sits down and does the one piece of analysis that finance teams almost never do:

- The analysis of what their latency is actually costing.
- That number, in most organisations, is large enough to change the conversation entirely.

In the next chapter, we will explore why even having read this far, most finance professionals will find it genuinely difficult to see this pattern in their own behaviour. The precision trap does not just cost organisations. It conceals itself from the very people who are most responsible for perpetuating it.

4

Why You Can't See It from the Inside

Let us pause for a moment before moving forward.

You have just read seven stories about finance teams whose work arrived too late.

A missed acquisition. Three years of underpricing. A CEO who quietly rerouted his decisions away from the function that existed to support them. A shadow analytics team built by a business unit that had simply stopped waiting. A billion-dollar budget made obsolete overnight by a pandemic. A $3.2 million pricing window that closed while the analysis was still being built. And an advertising agency that spent ninety days waiting for the perfect invoice when sixty percent of the cash could have been collected in thirty.

If you are a finance professional. And the chances are high that you are, given what you are reading this book. One of two things probably happened as you worked through those stories.

The first possibility is that you recognised them. Not abstractly, not intellectually, but viscerally with the specific sensation of seeing a pattern you have lived inside described from the outside for the first time. If that happens, this chapter will confirm what you already suspect about yourself and give you language for it.

The second possibility is more interesting, and more important.

The second possibility is that you read those stories and thought yes, but not us. We are different. When something genuinely urgent comes up, we move. We have a good relationship with the business. Our CEO trusts us. The precision trap is a real problem, but it is someone else's problem.

If that was your reaction, this chapter is written specifically for you.

Because that reaction, confident, well-intentioned, and entirely sincere is itself the most reliable symptom of the trap. The finance teams most deeply embedded in precision culture are almost never the ones who recognise themselves in descriptions of it. They are the ones who read those descriptions and think of a colleague in another organization, a team they heard about at a conference, a function they consulted for once that clearly had issues.

The trap does not announce itself. It does not feel like a trap from the inside. It feels like professionalism.

This chapter is about why.

THE COMPETENCE PARADOX

There is a deeply uncomfortable truth at the heart of the precision trap, and it is this: the most skilled finance professionals are often the most deeply embedded in it.

This is not intuitive. We tend to assume that capability and self-awareness travel together. And that better analysts are better at recognizing the limitations of their own approach. In most disciplines this is broadly true. But the precision trap operates differently, because skill itself becomes the mechanism of concealment.

Here is how it works.

A less experienced analyst, faced with a request for a quick directional view, will produce a quick directional view. Not because they have made a deliberate choice about accuracy versus speed. But because they do not yet have the technical capability to build anything more sophisticated in the available time. Their limitations enforce an appropriate response.

A highly skilled analyst, faced with the same request, sees immediately all the ways the quick answer could be improved. They know the working capital assumptions should be stress-tested. They know the comparable transactions data would strengthen the recommendation. They know the sensitivity table would make the conclusion more defensible. And they are right on all counts. Each of those additions would, in isolation, make the analysis technically better.

What their skill does not automatically provide is the judgement to ask whether technically better is what the situation requires. **Whether the decision that needs to be made actually needs a stress-tested working capital assumption, or whether it needs a clear directional answer by end of day. Whether the extra two days of work will change the recommendation, or whether it will simply make the analyst feel more confident in a recommendation that was already correct.**

The skilled analyst builds the more sophisticated analysis not because they have been asked to, and not because the decision requires it, but because they can. And because their professional identity is built around the quality of their work. Every additional layer of analysis feels like quality. The instinct to add it feels like conscientiousness.

From the outside this looks like latency. From the inside it feels like doing the job properly.

This is the competence paradox. The better you are at building precise analyses, the more naturally you gravitate toward building them regardless of whether the situation calls for them. Skill, without the accompanying judgement about when to deploy it, becomes a liability disguised as a strength.

The most dangerous finance professionals in an organization are not the incompetent ones. Those are visible and correctable. At times the most dangerous are the highly capable ones who have never been asked to think carefully about whether their capability is being applied in the right direction.

Daniel had been an FP&A manager for eight years when his commercial director asked him a question he thought he understood.

The company was considering pulling back from its third-largest customer. The relationship had been difficult for two years. Service complaints were rising. The account team was exhausted. The commercial director wanted to know if it made financial sense to walk away.

Daniel spent four days building the model. Revenue contribution. Margin by product line. Volume impact on fixed cost absorption. Replacement revenue scenarios. He stress-tested it across six assumptions and produced a clean, comprehensive analysis that concluded, with a high degree of confidence, that walking away would cost the company approximately $2.3 million in contribution margin in year one.

The commercial director read it carefully. Then she asked a question Daniel had not considered.

What does this customer cost us in management time?

Daniel did not have that number. It had never occurred to him to build it. Management time was not in the general ledger. It did not appear in any variance report. It could not be pulled from any system he had access to. It was, by every measure available to him, unmeasurable. So, he had not measured it.

What the commercial director knew, from conversations Daniel had never been part of, was that this single account consumed roughly thirty percent of the senior commercial team's bandwidth on chasing escalations, managing complaints, renegotiating terms that had already been agreed.

The opportunity cost of that attention, applied elsewhere, was orders of magnitude larger than the $2.3 million contribution margin the model had identified.

The decision had already been made before Daniel's analysis arrived. Not because the commercial director did not value finance's input. Because the question Daniel had answered, what this customer contributes, was not the question that needed answering.

The question that needed answering was in the dark. Daniel had searched where the light was. He had produced four days of technically excellent work about the wrong thing.

There is a name for this pattern that comes from outside finance entirely.

It is called the Streetlight Effect. A man loses his keys in a dark parking lot. A passerby finds him searching under a streetlight some distance away. Is that where you dropped them? the passerby asks. No, the man replies. But this is where the light is.

Finance teams do not search for the wrong insight because they are careless. They search where the light is, where the data is clean, where the models are established, where the analytical tools are familiar.

The question of whether the analysis is landing in time to matter is not where the light is. It is somewhere in the darker territory of decision impact, stakeholder trust, and analytical latency, concepts that have no line in any management account and no column in any performance review.

So, they are not examined. Not because they are unimportant. Because the profession has never built the tools to illuminate them. And what cannot be illuminated, in a culture trained to work only with numbers, tends not to exist.

The competence paradox and the streetlight effect operate together. Skill determines where you search. The streetlight determines what you find. A highly skilled finance professional searching in the wrong place will find nothing useful and will find it with extraordinary thoroughness.

THE IDENTITY PROBLEM

In the spring of their second year at a large consumer goods company, a newly promoted FP&A manager received a piece of feedback from their director that they still remember years later.

They had been asked to provide a quick view on a proposed marketing investment. A rough ROI, directional sense of whether the spend made sense. Knowing the director needed the answer quickly, they had turned around a single-page analysis in four hours. Clean, clear, well-argued. Directional, as requested.

The director's feedback was not what they expected.

This feels thin. I would have expected more rigor from you on something like this. We need to be able to defend our numbers.

The analyst never made that mistake again. Not the mistake of being too quick. The mistake of appearing insufficiently thorough. They learned, from a single piece of feedback, that speed without visible rigor was professionally risky. That a thin analysis, even a correct one, reflected badly on their capabilities. That the way to be respected in this function was to produce work that looked comprehensive, whatever the situation required.

They became excellent analysts. Thorough, rigorous, highly regarded. They were promoted several times over the following decade.

They also became someone who, by their own admission in a reflective moment many years later, had never once in their career explicitly asked a business leader how quickly they needed an answer before they had already begun building the most complete analysis they could produce.

This story is not unusual. It is, in its essential shape, the story of how precision culture reproduces itself in individuals. It is through feedback, through reward, through the gradual internalization of thoroughness as a component of professional identity.

By the time a finance professional reaches a senior level, the preference for comprehensive analysis is not a conscious choice they make on each piece of work. It is part of who they are. It is how they think about what good work means. It is bound up with their self-image as a capable, rigorous, trustworthy professional.

This is what makes the precision trap so resistant to correction through rational argument alone. You can show a finance leader the data on decision latency. You can walk them through the seven stories in chapter three. You can make the intellectual case clearly and compellingly. And they can agree with every word of it genuinely, sincerely. And still find it almost impossible to change their behaviour.

Because changing their behaviours does not feel like adopting a better professional practice. It feels like becoming a worse version of themselves.

The identity investment in thoroughness is real and it is deep. It was built over years of feedback, reward, and professional socialization. It does not dissolve in response to an argument, however well-made. It dissolves slowly, through repeated experience of doing things differently and finding that the world does not end. That the rough answer was good enough, that the business leader valued the speed, that the decision was better for having had financial input rather than worse for having had imprecise financial input.

That is a slow process. And it cannot begin until the finance professional can see the identity investment clearly enough to examine it.

Most never get that far. Because the feedback loops that would force that examination almost never activate.

THE MISSING FEEDBACK LOOP

We touched on this in Chapter Two. It is worth going deeper.

In most professional disciplines, mistakes generate consequences that are visible enough to correct behaviours over time.

A structural engineer whose calculations are wrong sees the building. A doctor whose diagnosis is incorrect sees the patient. A salesperson who loses a deal knows they lost it, knows approximately why, and has the opportunity to adjust their approach. The feedback is direct, proximate, and attributable. It lands on the person who made the error with enough clarity to produce learning.

Finance professionals exist in a fundamentally different feedback environment.

When an analysis arrives too late and a decision goes badly. Or goes less well than it might have. The causal chain between the latency and the outcome is almost never made explicit. The competitor moved faster. The market shifted. The timing was unfortunate. The executive who made the call on imperfect information might privately suspect that better financial input earlier would have helped. But they rarely say so. The post-mortem does not reach that conclusion. The lessons-learned document does not contain the line: finance was too slow, and this is what it cost.

So, the finance team receives no corrective signal. From their perspective, the analysis was thorough and well-received. The outcome was disappointing but for reasons unrelated to their work. There is nothing to learn, because nothing in the feedback they received suggested a problem.

This is not a small design flaw in the system. It is a structural feature that makes self-correction essentially impossible without deliberate intervention.

Consider what would need to be true for a finance team to naturally correct their latency through feedback alone. The business leader would need to explicitly attribute a bad outcome to slow financial analysis. The finance team would need to receive that attribution clearly and specifically. The performance management system would need to treat decision latency as a measurable failure rather than a non-event. And the individual analyst would need to connect their specific behaviours. The extra two days spent stress-testing assumptions to the specific cost that behaviours produced.

None of these things happen in normal organizational life. **Business leaders absorb the cost of late analysis without naming it. Finance teams receive feedback on output quality accuracy, completeness, presentation and not on decision impact. Performance management systems have no mechanism for measuring the value of analyses that were never delivered in time to matter.**

The finance professional who spends two extra days perfecting an analysis that arrives after the decision has been made does not receive negative feedback. They receive positive feedback, or no feedback at all. The analysis was good. The work was thorough. The outcome was disappointing but that was not finance's fault.

And so, they do it again. And again. And again.

Without a feedback loop that connects latency to cost, the behaviour that produces latency is perfectly rational from the perspective of the individual finance professional. They are doing exactly what their training, their identity, and their incentive structure tell them to do. They are being rigorous. They are being defensible. They are being professional.

They are just being professional in a way that the business cannot use.

WHAT THIS MEANS FOR CHANGE

Understanding these three mechanisms. The competence paradox, the identity investment, and the absent feedback loop matters because it explains why certain approaches to change do not work.

Telling finance teams, they need to move faster does not work. The message lands as a request to do worse work, which conflicts directly with the identity investment and produces resistance rather than change.

Showing finance teams data on decision latency does not work on its own. The intellectual case can be accepted entirely while the behaviours remain unchanged, because the behaviours is not driven by intellect. It is driven by identity and reinforced by feedback.

Restructuring reporting lines or implementing new technology does not work without addressing the underlying culture. You can give a precision-oriented finance team the fastest analytical tools in the world and they will use them to build more comprehensive analyses more quickly. The tool changes. The orientation does not.

So, what does work? And the following chapters will show this in detail. It is a combination of three things working simultaneously.

New metrics that create the feedback loop that is currently absent. You cannot correct behaviours that generates no negative signal. Creating explicit measures of decision impact like time to useful answer, percentage of analyses that changed a decision, stakeholder satisfaction with decision support gives the system the feedback mechanism it currently lacks.

New language that separates speed from sloppiness. The resistance to change is partly semantic. Finance professionals hear "move faster" as "be less rigorous." The reframe that calibrating precision to the decision is itself a form of rigor, that the most rigorous thing a finance team can do is ask what the decision needs before beginning the analysis. This gives professionals a way to change their behaviours without changing their identity. They are not becoming less thorough. They are becoming more precisely thorough.

New experiences that accumulate into new confidence. The identity investment in thoroughness was built through experience. Through the feedback, the rewards, and the professional socialization of years of finance work. It can only be rebuilt through experience. Through the repeated discovery that the rough answer was good enough, that the business leader valued the speed, that the decision was better for having finance involved rather than worse for having finance involved imprecisely. **One experience does not shift an identity. Twenty experiences, accumulated over months, begin to.**

None of this is quick. None of it is comfortable. And none of it can begin until the finance professional can look at their own work with sufficient honesty to ask the question that their training never asked them:

Was that analysis fast enough to be useful?

Not accurate enough. Not thorough enough. Not defensible enough.

Fast enough to be useful.

For many finance professionals, that question will feel wrong the first time they ask it. It will feel like a lowering of standards, a concession to impatience, a compromise of the professional values they have spent a career building.

Ask it anyway.

Because the answer, whatever it turns out to be is the beginning of escaping the trap.

The next chapter takes us somewhere that might, at first, seem like a detour.

We are going to look at the finance teams that never fell into the precision trap in the first place. Not because they were better trained or more self-aware, but because their circumstances gave them no choice.

The startup CFO, operating without the luxury of time or complete data, has been solving this problem by necessity for decades. What they know, and how they know it, turns out to be exactly what enterprise finance needs to learn deliberately.

5

The Startup CFO Exception

Sarah Chen had been CFO of a Series B fintech for fourteen months when she had the conversation that changed how she thought about her entire profession.

She was on a call with a former colleague. Someone she had worked alongside for three years at a large financial services firm before they had taken different paths. Her colleague had stayed. Sarah had left to join the startup. And her colleague, who was thoughtful and self-aware and genuinely curious about what the transition had been like, asked a question that Sarah found surprisingly difficult to answer.

Do you miss having proper data?

Sarah paused longer than she expected to.

The honest answer was complicated.

Yes, in one sense. She missed the clean systems, the complete data sets, the luxury of running a proper model with actual historical numbers behind it. At her previous employer she had known, to a high degree of confidence, what the next quarter would look like before it happened. The forecasting was good because the data was good and the business was stable and the patterns were reliable.

At fintech she was making consequential financial decisions. About runway, about hiring, about pricing, about which channels to invest in with data that was three months old, incomplete, sometimes contradictory, and occasionally wrong. She was operating at 60% information on a good day.

But here was the thing she struggled to explain to her colleague, who was still operating in the environment they had both come from.

She was faster. She was more useful. She was in more decisions, earlier, with more genuine influence over outcomes, than she had ever been in her previous role. And the decisions, the ones she was involved in with incomplete data and rough models and directional views rather than comprehensive analyses were not worse for her involvement. They were better.

I don't miss the data,* she finally said. *I miss feeling certain. But I've started to wonder whether the certainty was ever as useful as I thought it was.

THREE TYPES OF STARTUP CFO

Not every finance professional who ends up in a startup escapes the precision trap. The startup environment creates the conditions for escaping, the time pressure, the data scarcity, the direct accountability for business outcomes. But it does not guarantee it. How a finance leader responds to those conditions depends significantly on where they came from and what they bring with them.

In the startup world, three distinct types of finance leaders tend to emerge. Understanding them is useful not just as a taxonomy of startup finance but as a map of three different relationships with the precision trap, and what each one can teach enterprise finance.

THE OPERATOR CFO

The Operator CFO typically comes from a commercial or operational background before moving into finance, or has spent their entire career in high-growth environments where the luxury of complete data simply never existed.

They are comfortable genuinely, not performatively comfortable with 60% answers. Not because they do not care about accuracy, but because they have spent enough time in fast-moving businesses to have developed an intuitive calibration between the precision a decision requires and the precision that is actually available. They know, almost instinctively, when an analysis is good enough to act on and when it genuinely needs more work.

The Operator CFO does not experience rough answers as a compromise of their professional standards. They experience them as appropriate professional judgement. The same judgement a good doctor exercises when they make a clinical decision with incomplete test results because waiting for the results would cost the patient more than acting on the available evidence.

When an Operator CFO joins a company that is scaling toward enterprise size, one of two things happens. Either the culture they have built is strong enough to survive the growth and they bring decision velocity with them into the larger organization. Or the enterprise culture gradually absorbs them and the instincts that made them excellent in a startup environment get slowly eroded by the new environment's expectations of thoroughness and defensibility.

The latter happens more often than the former. Which is a significant loss, both for the individuals and for the organizations that hired them partly because of what those instincts represented.

THE IPO-TRACK CFO

The IPO-Track CFO is a different profile entirely. They have typically been brought into a scaling startup specifically to professionalize the finance function to build the systems, controls, and reporting frameworks that a company needs as it grows toward a liquidity event.

They come, more often than not, from investment banking, private equity, or the finance function of a larger company. They bring rigor, structure, and institutional credibility. They are excellent at building the infrastructure that a maturing company needs.

They are also, frequently, the first person in the organization to slow things down.

This is not always a problem. Some slowing down is appropriate and necessary as a company scales. The controls that felt like bureaucracy at twenty people feel like governance at two hundred. The CFO who insists on proper process is not always wrong.

But the IPO-Track CFO who applies enterprise precision standards to decisions that do not require them who builds the 40-slide deck for a question that needed a one-page answer, who runs the full sensitivity analysis on a decision that needed a directional view is importing the precision trap into an environment that had previously been free of it.

Founders who have worked with this type of CFO describe a specific and recognizable experience: the moment when they first felt like they needed finance's permission to move, rather than finance's support to move well. The transition from finance as an accelerant to finance as a process. The gradual replacement of speed with defensibility.

The best IPO-Track CFOs bring the rigor without bringing the trap. They know which decisions need the full institutional treatment and which ones need the startup instinct. They are bilingual fluent in both the language of enterprise governance and the language of decision velocity. They are also, for that reason, genuinely rare.

THE ACCIDENTAL CFO

The Accidental CFO did not plan to be in finance leadership. They were a strong financial analyst, or a capable controller, or an operations leader who was good with numbers and found themselves, through a combination of company growth and talent scarcity, elevated into a CFO role before they had developed a clear view of what that role should look like.

They default to what they know. And what they know, more often than not, is precision. Because precision is what finance training teaches. Precision is what was rewarded in every role they held before this one. Precision is the only professional standard they have ever been explicitly evaluated against.

The Accidental CFO in a startup is simultaneously the most common and the most instructive case. Because they enter a high-speed environment with a precision-oriented toolkit and are forced by the environment itself to develop new instincts. Not through deliberate professional development. Not through reading a book or attending a training program. But through the relentless pressure of a business that cannot wait and will not wait and makes clear, through the direct feedback of outcomes and relationships, that the toolkit needs to expand.

The Accidental CFO who survives this process and emerges on the other side is the most interesting finance leader in any room. They have both sets of instincts the rigor that their training built, and the velocity that their environment forced. They have, through experience rather than theory, solved the problem that this book is trying to help enterprise finance professionals solve deliberately.

When you find one of them, and ask them to describe how their thinking changed, the answer almost always contains the same elements. A specific moment of pressure. A decision that had to be made without complete information. The discovery that the decision was not worse for having been made that way. And the gradual, accumulated confidence that came from making twenty more decisions in the same way and finding, most of the time, that the outcome was fine.

WHAT THE STARTUP ENVIRONMENT ACTUALLY TEACHES

The three CFO types illustrate different paths through the same territory. But beneath those individual differences, the startup environment itself teaches a set of lessons that are worth extracting directly. Because they are the lessons that enterprise finance teams need most, and the ones that enterprise finance culture makes almost impossible to learn any other way.

LESSON ONE: DATA SCARCITY FORCES PRIORITIZATION

In an enterprise finance team, data is usually available. The question is not whether to include a data point but how much depth to go into each one. This creates a particular kind of analytical expansion the model gets larger not because it needs to be but because the data exists and therefore feels like it should be included.

In a startup, data scarcity is the norm. There is no five-year history to draw on. The customer data is incomplete. The market size figures are estimates. The competitive landscape is shifting. And the decision needs to be made this week.

This forces a discipline that enterprise finance rarely develops naturally the discipline of asking, before beginning any analysis, what are the two or three numbers that will actually determine this decision? Not what data is available. But what data matters? The distinction sounds simple. In practice it is the difference between a four-hour analysis and a four-week analysis that reaches the same conclusion.

LESSON TWO: SPEED BUILDS TRUST FASTER THAN ACCURACY

This is counterintuitive enough to be worth sitting with.

In enterprise finance, the conventional wisdom is that trust is built through accuracy through producing numbers that are right, models that hold up under scrutiny, analyses that cannot be challenged. The finance professional who is never wrong earns the trust of the business over time.

Startup CFOs discover something different. Trust, in a fast-moving business, is built through availability and usefulness. Through being the person who has a view when a view is needed. Through showing up to a conversation with a rough answer rather than a timeline for when the proper answer will be ready. Through demonstrating, repeatedly, that finance can be a thinking partner rather than a reporting function.

The finance leader who says I don't have the full picture yet but here is my directional read and here is what would change. Now that earns more trust, faster, than the finance leader who says give me a week and I will have something comprehensive for you. Not because the rough answer is better than the comprehensive one. But because the rough answer is there when the conversation is happening, and the comprehensive answer arrives after the conversation has moved on.

LESSON THREE: BEING WRONG QUICKLY IS BETTER THAN BEING RIGHT SLOWLY

Enterprise finance culture is deeply risk-averse about being wrong. The professional cost of an analysis that turns out to be incorrect is felt immediately and attributed directly. The professional cost of an analysis that arrives too late is diffuse and rarely attributed at all.

This asymmetry produces a rational individual preference for slowness. Being slow and right is safe. Being fast and wrong is risky.

Startup environments break this asymmetry through a different feedback structure. In a high-growth company with monthly board meetings, weekly leadership reviews, and daily commercial decisions, the cost of slowness is visible and immediate. The CEO who cannot get a financial view in time to make a decision notices. The board that receives a forecast two weeks after the quarter has already developed different notices. The commercial team that cannot get a pricing recommendation before the customer conversation notices.

This visibility of the cost of slowness changes the calculus. Suddenly being slow and right is not safe; it is just slow. And being fast and roughly right, with an explicit acknowledgement of the uncertainty in the number, is not risky, it is useful.

The startup CFO who has internalized this lesson brings something invaluable to any organization they subsequently join. A lived understanding that the professional risk of speed is lower than the professional risk of latency, once you are operating in an environment where latency has a visible cost.

THE TRANSLATION PROBLEM

Here is the challenge that makes this chapter more than an interesting observation about startup finance.

The lessons that startup CFOs learn by necessity are the same lessons that enterprise finance teams need to learn deliberately. The instincts that the startup environment forces are the instincts that enterprise finance culture actively suppresses. The behaviours that build trust in a fast-moving organization are the behaviours that get penalized in a slow-moving one.

And the finance professionals who have learned those lessons: the Operator CFOs, the Accidental CFOs who survived their startup environments, the bilingual IPO-Track CFOs who can move between registers exist in significant numbers. They are in the market. Some of them are already in enterprise finance roles, their startup instincts gradually eroding under the pressure of the new environment.

The question for enterprise finance leaders is not whether the knowledge exists. It is whether the culture they are operating in allows that knowledge to be expressed.

A finance professional who spent four years in a Series B and learned to deliver directional views in four hours will deliver directional views in four hours when the situation calls for it right up until the first time their manager tells them the work feels thin. After that, they will build the 40-slide deck like everyone else.

The environment shapes the behaviour. Not once, but continuously. The startup CFO who joins a large organization does not carry their startup instincts indefinitely against the pressure of the new culture. They adapt or they leave.

This is why the solution to the precision trap is not, primarily, a hiring problem. Hiring faster finance professionals into a precision culture produces slower finance professionals within eighteen months. The culture wins. It always wins, unless something more fundamental changes.

What needs to change and the following chapters will show exactly how it is the environment itself. The metrics, the language, the feedback loops, and the explicit expectations that define what good finance work looks like in a particular organization.

When those things change, the startup instincts that enterprise finance professionals already have are the ones that were trained out of them, or never developed because the environment never required them to have somewhere to go.

Dr. Jason Fung's thermostat again, the one we met earlier, now operating on a finance team instead of on the body. The team has a set point it defends. An individual who tries to override it on willpower alone loses the same way a dieter loses to their own metabolism. The environment wins until the setting itself is changed.

This is why hiring a startup CFO into a precision culture produces a precision CFO within eighteen months. It is not weakness or lack of conviction. It is the thermostat working exactly as designed. The new hire cuts the calories: delivers faster, more directional answers and the culture fights back until the behaviour reverts.

The solution is not a faster finance professional. It is a reset thermostat. And resetting a thermostat requires changing the setting itself: the metrics, the feedback loops, the language of what good work looks like and not simply applying more willpower to the existing one. That is what Part Three of this book is about.

THE BRIDGE

Sarah Chen, the fintech CFO from the opening of this chapter, eventually left her startup role to join a large consumer business as their Group FP&A Director. She was hired partly because of her startup experience. The CEO wanted someone who could move fast and think commercially.

Eighteen months in, she found herself in a familiar situation. A business unit leader needed a view on a market entry. He needed it by the end of the week. She had started building the analysis on Monday.

By Wednesday she had something directional, well-reasoned, and clear. It would have taken her four hours in her startup. It had taken her two days in this environment, partly because the data systems were more complex and partly because she had, without fully noticing, started building to the standard the culture expected rather than the standard the decision required.

She sent it on Wednesday afternoon with a note: ***This is directional and confidence level around 75%. Let me know if you need me to go deeper on any section, but I think this is enough to make the call.***

The business unit leader replied within an hour. *This is exactly what I needed. Thank you.*

Her manager, who saw the analysis in passing, stopped by her desk the following morning. *That felt a bit light for something of this size,* he said. *Next time let's make sure we have the full picture before we go out with something.*

Sarah recognised the moment. She had lived it before, from the other side. She understood exactly what was happening and exactly what it would cost if she adapted her behaviour in response to that single piece of feedback.

She also understood, for the first time with complete clarity, that changing this was not her problem to solve alone. It was the organizations.

That recognition that the precision trap is a cultural problem, not an individual one is where Part Two begins.

The framework that follows is not a set of personal productivity tips for individual finance professionals. It is a set of tools for changing the environment itself. The metrics, the language, the expectations, and the conversations that determine what good finance work looks like in any organization that is serious about escaping the trap.

6

The Three Questions That Change Everything

On a Tuesday morning, a finance business partner at a mid-sized professional services firm received a message from her commercial director.

Can you pull together the revenue numbers for the Henderson account? I need it as soon as possible.

She opened her laptop, navigated to the data system, and started pulling. By 11am she had a clean, well-structured Excel file monthly revenue for the past eighteen months, year on year comparisons, a variance analysis, and a short commentary explaining the three main movements in the numbers. It was accurate, thorough, and professional.

She sent it across at 11.15am.

The commercial director replied forty minutes later.

Thanks, this is great but I actually needed something I could show the client this afternoon. Can you put it in a slide? Something visual, just the headline numbers, nothing too detailed.

She rebuilt it. A clean one-pager, the key revenue figures, a simple chart, a headline message. It took another hour and a half. She sent it at 1pm. The commercial director used it in the client meeting at 3pm.

The Excel file: eighteen months of data, variance analysis, commentary was never opened again.

Two hours of work. Rendered unnecessary by one question that was never asked.

Of all the habits that separate good finance business partners from great ones, the most important is also the most consistently overlooked. It does not require technical skill. It does not require seniority or confidence or years of experience. It requires thirty seconds and a single message before opening any data system or touching any spreadsheet.

It requires asking "why?"

Not why in the philosophical sense. Not a challenge or a pushback or a request for justification. A simple, specific, practical question asked before any analysis begins. What is this for, who needs it, and when does it actually need to be ready?

Those three questions Why, who, when are the foundation of Decision Tiering.

And Decision Tiering is the first and most important tool for escaping the precision trap, because it addresses the problem at its source. Not after the analysis has been built. Not after the deck has been delivered. Before a single Excel file has been opened or a single number pulled.

The finance professional who asks those three questions before starting will build the right analysis almost every time. The finance professional who does not ask them will build a thorough, accurate, professionally rigorous analysis that is wrong for the situation with a frequency that would alarm them if they ever stopped to count.

THE MOMENT NOBODY TALKS ABOUT

There is a specific moment in the working life of every finance professional that determines more about their effectiveness than almost any other. It is not the moment they present to the board. It is not the moment they close the month. It is not the moment they deliver the forecast or defend the budget or explain the variance.

It is the moment a request arrives.

An email. A Slack message. A question asked in passing at the end of a meeting. A voice note from a business partner who needs something before the end of the day.

In that moment in the few seconds between receiving the request and deciding what to do next. A finance professional makes a set of decisions that will determine everything about the analysis that follows. How deep it goes. What format it takes. How long it takes to build. Whether it lands correctly or needs to be rebuilt.

And in the vast majority of cases, those decisions are made without the one piece of information that would make them correct. An understanding of what the analysis is actually for.

Watch what happens at that moment in most finance teams. The request arrives. The finance professional reads it. And then they open Excel. Or they navigate to the data system. Or they start pulling the numbers that the request mentioned.

They have answered a question before asking one.

They have decided implicitly, instinctively, without conscious deliberation what the output needs to look like, how deep it needs to go, and how long it deserves. And they have made that decision based on the content of the request rather than the purpose behind it.

This is the most expensive habit in finance. Not because it produces bad analysis. Because it produces the wrong analysis thoroughly, accurately, and precisely calibrated to a need that was assumed rather than understood.

WHY THE SAME REQUEST NEEDS TWO COMPLETELY DIFFERENT RESPONSES

Here is the thing about finance requests that makes this habit so costly.

The same request, from the same person, about the same numbers, can require two completely different analytical responses depending on a single variable. What is it for?

Consider the revenue number.

A business partner sends a message: *can you pull the revenue numbers for the Henderson account?*

If that request is for a QBR a quarterly business review with the internal leadership team what is needed is depth. Historical trends, year on year movements, variance analysis, commentary on the drivers, context for the numbers. The audience is internal, financially literate, and wants to understand what is happening and why. The output is probably an Excel file or a detailed slide with supporting data. It needs to be thorough because the people in that room will ask detailed questions and the finance professional needs to be able to answer them.

If that request is for a client call. A meeting with the Henderson account itself. What is needed is something completely different. A clean visual. Headline numbers. A simple narrative. Nothing that looks like internal management accounting. The audience is external, the relationship is commercial, and the output needs to build confidence rather than answer analytical questions. Depth is not just unnecessary. It is actively counterproductive. A client shown an internal variance analysis with commentary on the drivers will feel like they are being shown something they were not supposed to see.

Same request. Same data. Completely different output.

The finance professional who builds the Excel file with eighteen months of data and a variance analysis for a client call has not done bad work. They have done the wrong work competently, thoroughly, and entirely unnecessarily.

And the only way to know which one to build is to ask.

Priya had been a finance business partner for five years when she received a message that seemed, on the surface, entirely straightforward.

Her head of supply chain sent her a short note on a Monday morning. Can you pull together a cost analysis of our top twenty suppliers? Need it as soon as possible.

Priya knew exactly what to do. She had built supplier cost analyses before. She opened her laptop, navigated to the procurement database, and began pulling. By Wednesday afternoon she had a comprehensive breakdown: unit costs, volume discounts, logistics costs, payment terms, three-year trend analysis, and a benchmarking comparison against industry averages. It was accurate, thorough, and professionally structured. She sent it across at 4pm.

The head of supply chain replied the following morning.

This is great work. Actually, what I needed was something much simpler. Just the top five suppliers by spend with a rough sense of whether we are getting a fair price. I have a board meeting on Friday and I need one slide.

Priya rebuilt it in two hours. A clean single page. Five suppliers. Three data points each. A headline recommendation. The comprehensive analysis: two and a half days of careful work was never opened again.

She mentioned it to a colleague over lunch that Friday. Her colleague asked a question she had not considered.

Did you ask him what it was for before you started?

Priya paused. She had not. The request had seemed clear. Supplier cost analysis. She knew how to build one. So, she had built one. What she had never asked was why.

There is a framework that Toyota built into the foundation of its entire manufacturing philosophy. It is called the 5 Whys. When something goes wrong on the production line, the engineer does not fix what is visible. They ask why it happened. Then they ask why that happened. Then they ask why again. Five times, until they reach the cause beneath the cause beneath the cause, the root of the problem rather than its surface expression.

Taiichi Ohno, the architect of the Toyota Production System, used a simple example to illustrate it. A machine stopped working. Why? Because it was overloaded. Why? Because the bearing was not lubricated. Why? Because the pump was not working. Why? Because the shaft was worn. Why? Because there was no strainer and metal scrap got in. Five whys. One root cause. A completely different solution than the one the surface symptom suggested.

Finance teams that receive a request and immediately open Excel are fixing the surface symptom. They are answering the question as stated rather than the question that matters. The revenue numbers for the Henderson account is just the surface. The client call at 3pm is the root. Asking why, who, and when before touching any data is the finance professional's equivalent of the 5 Whys. It is the discipline of not solving the problem that presents itself until you understand the problem that actually exists. It takes thirty seconds. But it is so powerful that it changes everything that follows.

THE THREE QUESTIONS

Decision Tiering is built on three questions. They take thirty seconds to ask. They can be asked on Slack, by email, in a voice note, or in a ten second conversation in the corridor. There is no situation in which they cannot be asked and no request for which they are not relevant.

QUESTION ONE: WHY DO YOU NEED IT?

What decision does this analysis support? What will the person asking do differently depending on what the numbers show? Is this for a meeting, a decision, a presentation or a negotiation? Is it to inform or to persuade? Is it internal or external?

The answer to these questions determines the purpose of the analysis. And purpose determines everything: depth, format, tone, and the level of precision that is actually required.

QUESTION TWO: WHO IS ASKING?

Not who sent the message: who is the ultimate audience for this work? Is it the person who asked, or are they passing it up to someone more senior? Is it a client, a board member, a CEO, a department head, a junior manager? Is it one person or a room full of people?

The answer to this question determines the format and the register. A CFO needs a different output than a commercial director. A client needs a different output than an internal leadership team. A board needs a different output than a department head. The numbers might be identical. The way they are presented, the depth of supporting analysis, and the language used to explain them will be completely different.

QUESTION THREE: WHEN DO YOU ACTUALLY NEED IT?

Not when you would ideally like it. When does the decision actually need to be made? Is there a meeting at 3pm today or is this for something next week? Is the deadline real or is it the assumed deadline that appears on every request regardless of actual urgency?

The answer to this question determines the appropriate investment of time and analytical depth. A decision that needs to be made in four hours requires a different analytical response than a decision that needs to be made in four days even if the underlying question is identical. Four hours means directional and clear. Four days means there is room for depth if the decision genuinely requires it.

Three questions. Why, who, when. Asked before any data is pulled or any model is opened. The answers determine everything about the right analytical response.

This is Decision Tiering in its simplest form. The practice of classifying a decision before beginning the analysis, so that the analysis is calibrated to what the decision actually needs rather than what the finance professional assumes it needs.

THE REAL REASON FINANCE PROFESSIONALS DON'T ASK

If three questions asked in thirty seconds can prevent hours of misdirected work, the obvious question is why finance professionals do not ask them consistently.

The answer is not laziness. It is not arrogance. It is not a lack of awareness that the questions would be useful.

For many finance professionals and this is something that almost never gets named in finance training or leadership development the real barrier is shyness.

Finance attracts a disproportionate number of introverted, analytically oriented professionals who are more comfortable with numbers than with people, more comfortable producing work than initiating conversations, more comfortable demonstrating capability through output than through dialogue.

For these professionals and there are many of them, at every level of seniority asking a clarifying question before starting work feels socially risky in a way that is difficult to articulate but genuinely inhibiting. It feels like admitting you did not understand the request. It feels like bothering someone who is busy. It feels like the kind of question a junior person asks, not the kind of question a senior professional ask. It feels, in the culture of finance where capability is demonstrated through thoroughness, like a display of uncertainty rather than a demonstration of judgement.

So, they do not ask. They make assumptions. They build the most comprehensive version of the analysis they can produce and hope it lands correctly.

Sometimes it does. Often it does not.

The solution to this is not a motivational argument about the importance of asking questions. Telling an introverted finance professional that they should be more comfortable initiating conversations does not make them more comfortable initiating conversations. It just adds a layer of self-criticism to the existing discomfort.

The solution is a script.

Not a formal process or a structured framework that needs to be learned and practiced. A single message casual, specific, and safe that any finance professional can send in fifteen seconds without it feeling like a significant social act.

Something like this. *Hey Quick Question: the revenue numbers you asked for, is it for the QBR review or a client call?*

That is it. Eleven words. Casual enough that it does not feel like a formal clarifying process. Specific enough that it gets a useful answer. Safe enough that an introverted finance professional can send it without feeling exposed.

Quick question is the linguistic key. It signals that this is not a challenge or a pushback or a request for justification. It is a colleague checking in before diving in. It takes the social weight out of the task entirely.

The finance professional who sends that message before opening Excel will within a week, wonder how they ever started an analysis without it. Because the answer they get back: QBR or client call, internal or external, today or next week changes everything about what they build next. And building the right thing the first time is faster, less stressful, and more professionally rewarding than building the wrong thing thoroughly and then rebuilding it correctly under time pressure.

WHAT CHANGES WHEN FINANCE TEAMS ASK

The transformation that happens when a finance team consistently asks why, who, and when before starting any analysis is visible enough that the business notices it. Even if they cannot immediately articulate what is different.

What they notice first is that the outputs land correctly. The analysis that arrives is the analysis that was needed not more, not less, not in the wrong format, not calibrated to the wrong audience. The commercial director gets the one-pager for the client meeting. The

CFO gets the detailed model for the board. The department head gets the Excel file for the QBR. First time, every time.

This sounds like a small thing. It is not. Every time an analysis lands incorrectly and needs to be rebuilt, something more than time is lost. A small amount of trust is lost. The business partner who receives the wrong output, however technically excellent, registers, consciously or unconsciously, that finance did not quite understand what they needed. That registration accumulates. Over months and years, it shapes the business partner's view of finance as a function useful for certain things, not quite right for others, better to do yourself if you need it quickly and correctly.

The finance team that consistently delivers the right output first time builds a completely different reputation. Not the reputation of a technically excellent function. The reputation of a function that understands the business. That gets it. That can be trusted to produce something useful rather than something thorough.

That reputation built one correctly calibrated output at a time is the foundation of genuine finance business partnering. Not the ability to build sophisticated models or present to the board or understand complex accounting standards. The ability to understand what is needed before building it.

For the finance professionals themselves the transformation is equally significant and more immediately felt.

Less stress. Because the analysis they are building is the right one. There is no background anxiety about whether the output will land correctly, no creeping sense halfway through the model that this might not be what was actually needed. The purpose is clear. The output is calibrated. The work feels purposeful rather than speculative.

More confidence. Because asking why, who, and when before starting is itself a demonstration of judgement, the judgement to understand that the right analysis depends on the right context. Business partners who receive the "Quick Question" message do not think less of the finance professional who sent it. They think more of them. The question signals that this is someone who thinks before they build. That is rare enough to be noticed.

Better feedback. Because the output lands correctly, the feedback reflects the quality of the work rather than the mismatch between what was built and what was needed. Finance professionals who consistently ask the three questions consistently receive feedback that their work is useful, relevant, and well-calibrated because it is.

Less rework. Which is perhaps the most immediately valuable benefit for a profession that spends an extraordinary amount of its time rebuilding analyses that were right in every technical sense but wrong for the situation. ***The finance professional who asks why before starting builds the right thing once. The finance professional who does not ask builds the wrong thing, receives a redirect, and builds the right thing second time. Same output. Double the time. Half the professional satisfaction.***

THE DEEPER SHIFT

There is something more significant happening when a finance professional consistently asks those three questions than a simple improvement in output quality.

They are shifting their orientation from production to partnership.

The finance professional who opens Excel the moment a request arrives is oriented toward production. Their job, as they understand it, is to produce accurate analysis in response to requests. The request is the input. The analysis is the output. The quality of the work is measured by the technical accuracy of the output.

The finance professional who asks why, who, and when before touching any data is oriented toward partnership. Their job, as they understand it, is to support a decision. The request is not the input; the decision is the input. The analysis is not the output; the decision is the output. The quality of the work is measured not by the technical accuracy of the analysis but by the usefulness of the decision it supported.

That shift from production to partnership, from output to outcome, from analysis to decision is the shift that finance business partnering has been trying to describe for two decades without ever quite landing on the mechanism that makes it happen.

The mechanism is three questions asked before opening Excel.

Why? Who? When?

Thirty seconds that change the orientation of the entire analytical effort that follows. Thirty seconds that separate the finance professional who produces accurate work from the finance professional who produces useful work. Thirty seconds that, accumulated across fifty requests a year, across an entire career, determine whether a finance professional is remembered as technically excellent or genuinely indispensable.

The "Quick Question" message is not a communication technique. It is a philosophy made practical. It is the moment a finance professional stops asking themselves. How do I answer this question? and starts asking what does this decision need?

That is the question that escapes the precision trap.

And it fits in eleven words on Slack or Microsoft teams.

In the next chapter, we take the insight from this one step further. Knowing the purpose of an analysis tells you what to build.

The Accuracy Dial tells you how much of it to build and introduces the concept that will feel most uncomfortable to precision-oriented finance professionals: that there is such a thing as too much accuracy, and that knowing when you have reached it is one of the most valuable judgments a finance professional can develop.

7

The Accuracy Dial

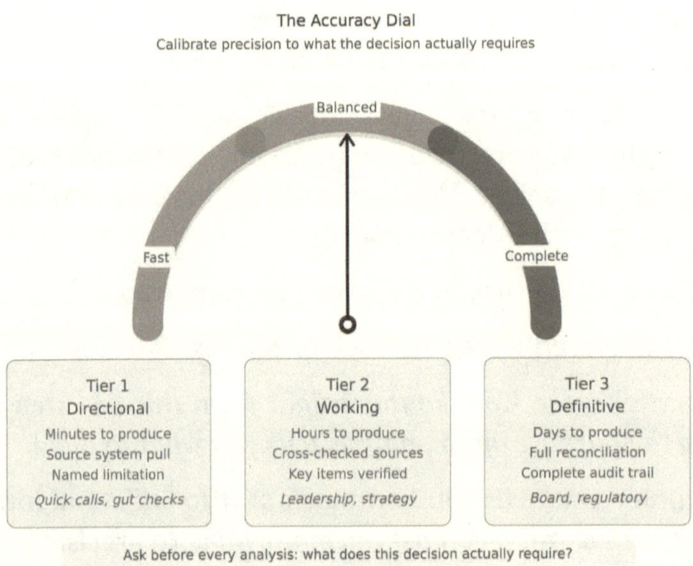

On a Wednesday afternoon, a senior finance business partner at a global banking group received a message from her commercial director.

"Can you get me the revenue figures for the Meridian portfolio? I need it for a conversation this afternoon."

She knew what this meant. The commercial director had a client meeting at 4pm. He needed something clean, presentable, and directionally accurate. He did not need a fully reconciled number tied back to every sub-ledger in the general ledger. He needed a number he could speak to confidently in a room with a client.

She also knew something else. In her organization a regulated financial institution where precision was not a cultural preference but a legal requirement the instinct of every finance professional was to treat every number request as a regulatory submission. Full reconciliation. Complete audit trail. Every line is tied back to the source system.

She had learned by over years of watching analyses arrive too late to be useful, that this instinct entirely appropriate for the quarterly regulatory return was actively harmful when applied to a client conversation happening in three hours.

She pulled the number from the data warehouse. Checked it against the planning system for reasonableness. Sent it across in twenty minutes with a single line of caveat.

Revenue for Meridian as of yesterday close (the data warehouse figures, overnight refresh, not reconciled to GL). Directional only. Let me know if you need the fully reconciled number and I can have it by tomorrow morning.

The commercial director replied in four minutes.

Perfect. Exactly what I needed.

The fully reconciled number was never requested.

THE DEFAULT THAT NOBODY CHOSE

Every finance team has a default accuracy setting. And in almost every finance team that default is the same.

One hundred percent.

Not because anyone decided it should be. Not because every decision the finance team supports requires it. Not because the business partners who receive the analyses have asked for it or need it or would notice the difference between a 97% accurate number and a 100% accurate number in the context of the decisions they are making.

Because it is the only standard finance professionals have ever been trained to meet.

From the first day of an accounting qualification to the last performance review before retirement, finance professionals are evaluated on a single dimension of output quality which is accuracy. The number is right or it is wrong. The reconciliation ties or it does not. The audit trail is complete or it has gaps. There is no professional framework, no training program, no performance management system in the finance world that teaches professionals to ask a different question entirely.

How accurate does this actually need to be?

That question which is simple, practical, and useful than almost any other question a finance professional can ask before beginning an analysis is almost never asked. The answer is assumed. It is always one hundred percent. It has always been one hundred percent. It will always be one hundred percent because that is what finance does.

The Accuracy Dial is the practice of asking that question deliberately, before touching any data or opening any model, and calibrating the analytical response to what the decision actually requires rather than what the finance professional's training tells them to default to.

The name will feel strange at first. Finance professionals do not think of accuracy as something to be calibrated to context. That discomfort is exactly the point.

It is not a license for sloppiness. It is not permission to guess. It is not an argument that accuracy does not matter.

It is the recognition that accuracy exists on a spectrum, that different decisions sit at different points on that spectrum, and that the finance professional who understands where a given decision sits and builds accordingly is more useful, more trusted, and more effective than the one who defaults to one hundred percent regardless of context.

THE COST OF THE DEFAULT

Before introducing the framework, it is worth being precise about what the one hundred percent default actually costs.

In most finance teams, the final twenty to thirty percent of the time spent on any analysis goes into a specific set of activities. Checks and balances. Tying every number back to the source system. Reconciling every line to the general ledger. Building the complete audit trail that ensures no number in the analysis can be challenged under any circumstances by anyone.

These activities feel like rigor. They feel professionalism. They feel like doing the job properly.

They are not rigor. They are insurance.

The distinction matters. Rigor means making sure the numbers that drive the decision are right. Insurance means making sure every number in the analysis is defensible against any possible challenge. Rigor serves the decision. Insurance serves the analyst.

The finance professional spending the final three hours of an analysis tying every number back to the system is not making the decision better. They are making themselves feel safer. They are building a defense against a challenge that may never come, in a conversation that may never happen, about a number that will not change the decision regardless of whether it is reconciled to the penny or to the nearest thousand.

And the cost of that insurance is the three hours, the delayed delivery, and the analysis that arrives after the conversation has already moved on is paid by the business, not by the analyst.

Across a team of five finance professionals, each running two analyses a week, twenty to thirty percent of total analytical effort going into checks and balances that do not change a single decision represents roughly one full person's time. Not spent generating insight. Not spent understanding the business. Not spent thinking about what the numbers mean and what the decision should be.

Spent reconciling.

That is the cost of the default. And it is a cost that almost never appears in any conversation about finance team productivity, because the activities that produce it look from the outside, exactly like the rigorous professional work that finance are supposed to be doing.

THE THREE TIERS

The Accuracy Dial framework organises analytical responses into three tiers. Not as a rigid classification system that must be applied formally to every request but as a way of making visible the spectrum that currently exists without being named, so that finance professionals can make a conscious choice about where on that spectrum a given analysis belongs.

TIER ONE: THE DIRECTIONAL NUMBER

The directional number is pulled from the most accessible authoritative source available the CRM, the data warehouse, the planning system and delivered quickly, with the source and its known limitations named explicitly.

It is not a guess. It is not an estimate constructed from assumptions or pulled from memory. It is a real number from a real system, delivered with a clear statement of what that system is, what its refresh cycle is, and what the known gap between that number and a fully reconciled figure might be.

The directional number takes minutes to produce, not hours. It is appropriate for client conversations, quick internal questions, directional reads on whether a proposal makes commercial sense, and any situation where the decision being made does not require precision beyond what the source system provides.

The language that accompanies it is not apologetic. It is confident and specific.

- *The number is from Salesforce: one day lag.*
- *Data warehouse figures: overnight refresh, not reconciled to GL.*
- *This is from the planning system: last updated Monday, so it does not include this week's movements.*

Each of those statements does the same thing. It names the source. It quantifies the limitation. It demonstrates that the finance professional knows their data architecture well enough to explain exactly what the number is and what it is not. That is not a weakness. That is expertise.

TIER TWO: THE WORKING NUMBER

The working number sits between the directional pull and the full reconciliation. It has been cross-checked against more than one source, verified for reasonableness, and carries a higher degree of confidence than a raw system pull but it has not been fully tied back to the general ledger or subjected to complete audit trail verification.

In practice, the working number often looks like:

- Last month's closed management accounts figure fully reconciled at the time of closing, not updated for subsequent movements, but reliable enough for most internal strategic and commercial decisions or
- A data warehouse figure that has been cross-referenced against the planning system and found to be within an acceptable range. or
- A CRM number that has been verified against the ERP for the key accounts that represent the majority of the revenue.

The working number takes hours, not days. It is appropriate for internal strategic discussions, leadership team reviews, commercial proposals, and decisions where the audience is financially literate and the stakes are significant but do not require regulatory-grade precision.

The caveat that accompanies it is similarly specific.

This is based on closed management accounts through last month and does not include March movements.

Cross-checked against planning and ERP for the top ten accounts, which represent 80% of the total. The tail has not been fully reconciled.

TIER THREE: THE DEFINITIVE NUMBER

The definitive number is the fully reconciled, completely verified, audit-trail-intact figure that finance professionals' default to producing for everything, regardless of whether everything requires it.

It is appropriate for regulatory submissions, statutory accounts, board-level acquisition decisions, external reporting, and any situation where the number will be scrutinized by an external authority or where the consequence of being wrong is significant enough to justify the full investment of time and effort.

It takes days, not hours. And it should be reserved for the decisions that genuinely require it which are fewer than the finance professional's default setting assumes, and more than zero.

The three tiers are not a rigid hierarchy. They are a vocabulary a set of named options that currently exist in practice but have never been made explicit enough to be chosen deliberately. The finance professional who understands all three knows, for any given request, which tier the decision sits in. And they build accordingly.

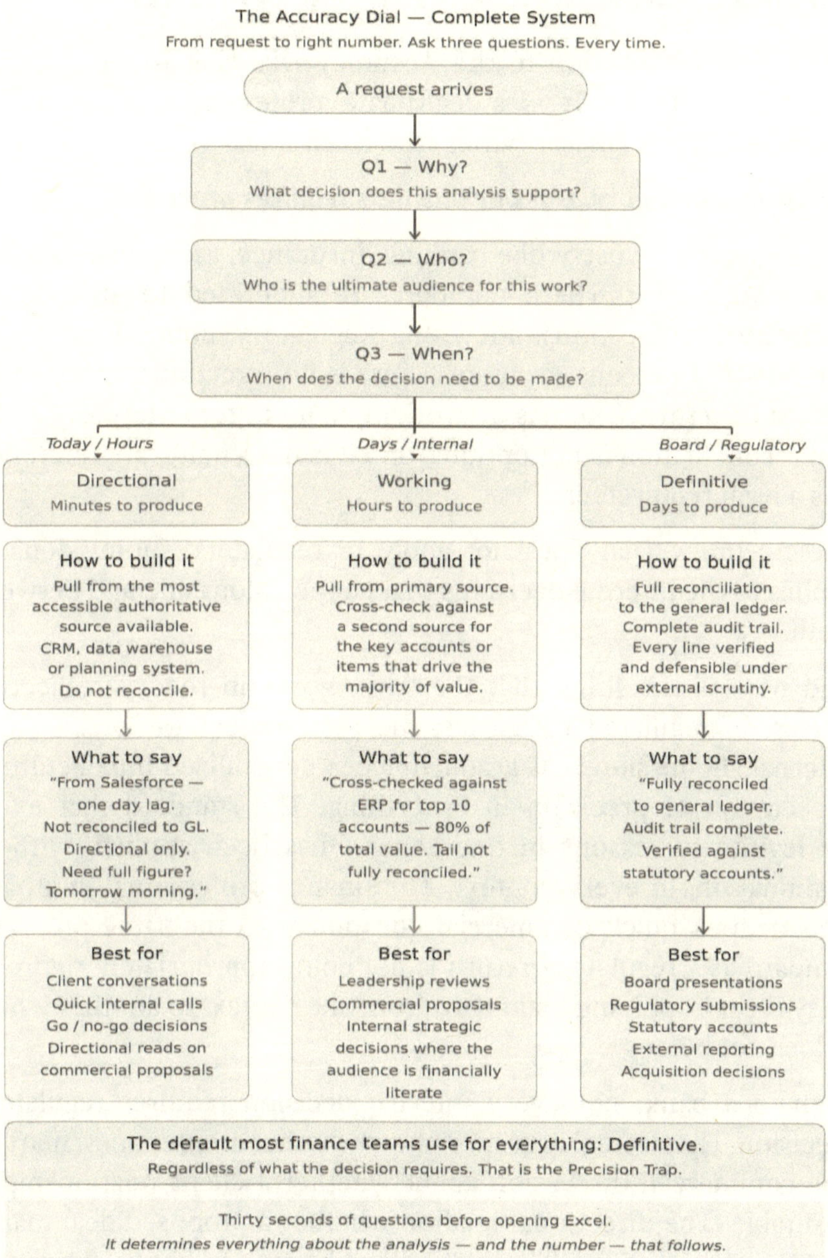
The Accuracy Dial — Complete System
From request to right number. Ask three questions. Every time.
A request arrives
Q1 — Why?
What decision does this analysis support?
Q2 — Who?
Who is the ultimate audience for this work?
Q3 — When?
When does the decision need to be made?
Today / Hours
Days / Internal
Board / Regulatory
Directional
Minutes to produce
Working
Hours to produce
Definitive
Days to produce
How to build it
Pull from the most accessible authoritative source available. CRM, data warehouse or planning system. Do not reconcile.
How to build it
Pull from primary source. Cross-check against a second source for the key accounts or items that drive the majority of value.
How to build it
Full reconciliation to the general ledger. Complete audit trail. Every line verified and defensible under external scrutiny.
What to say
"From Salesforce — one day lag. Not reconciled to GL. Directional only. Need full figure? Tomorrow morning."
What to say
"Cross-checked against ERP for top 10 accounts — 80% of total value. Tail not fully reconciled."
What to say
"Fully reconciled to general ledger. Audit trail complete. Verified against statutory accounts."
Best for
Client conversations
Quick internal calls
Go / no-go decisions
Directional reads on commercial proposals
Best for
Leadership reviews
Commercial proposals
Internal strategic decisions where the audience is financially literate
Best for
Board presentations
Regulatory submissions
Statutory accounts
External reporting
Acquisition decisions
The default most finance teams use for everything: Definitive.
Regardless of what the decision requires. That is the Precision Trap.
Thirty seconds of questions before opening Excel.
It determines everything about the analysis — and the number — that follows.

THE OBJECTION THAT DESERVES A DIRECT ANSWER

There is one objection to the Accuracy Dial that is more than a cultural resistance. It is a legitimate professional concern that deserves a direct answer rather than a reframe.

This works in theory. But our business requires precision.

In a regulated industry like banking, insurance, asset management, any environment where numbers are submitted to an external authority this objection is not wrong. Regulatory submissions require one hundred percent accuracy. There is no directional number for a Basel III return. There is no working number for a statutory audit. Full reconciliation is not optional and it is not a cultural preference. It is a legal requirement.

The Accuracy Dial does not apply to regulatory submissions. It applies to the internal decisions that happen alongside and between them.

And here is the thing that the "this works in theory" objection misses: in regulated industries, the requirement for precision in external submissions has gradually been generalized into a cultural expectation of precision in everything. The standard that exists for legitimate reasons in one context has been applied, without examination, to every context. The finance professional in a bank who treats a quick commercial question with the same precision standard as a regulatory return is not being appropriately rigorous. They are misapplying a standard from one context to another where it does not belong.

Even in a bank, not every internal decision requires regulatory precision. The strategic question about whether to enter a new market. The commercial discussion about whether a client relationship is profitable. The directional read on whether a proposed deal makes rough financial sense. These decisions happen in banks every day. They do not require the same precision standard as the quarterly regulatory return. And treating them as if they are defaulting to full reconciliation for every internal question because full reconciliation is required for external reporting is the precision trap operating at its most expensive.

The Accuracy Dial does not ask finance professionals in regulated industries to lower their standards. It asks them to apply the right standard to the right context. Which is, in itself, the more rigorous and more professional approach.

THE LANGUAGE OF APPROPRIATE PRECISION

One of the practical barriers to applying the Accuracy Dial is linguistics. Finance professionals who have been trained to deliver fully reconciled numbers do not have a natural vocabulary for delivering numbers that are less than fully reconciled without feeling like they are apologizing for incomplete work.

The solution is the same as in chapter six. Not a motivation script.

The language of appropriate precision is not apologetic. It is confident, specific, and demonstrates data literacy rather than concealing limitations. It does not say I only had time to pull a rough number. It says this is from the data warehouse, overnight refresh, not reconciled to GL. The first version sounds like a shortcut. The second version sounds like someone who knows exactly what their systems do and can explain it clearly.

Here are the specific forms that language takes in practice.

When delivering a Tier One directional number, name the system and the known lag.

Examples:

- *The number is from the billing system: overnight refresh.*
- *This is the bank feed: as at this morning, unreconciled.*
- *Headcount is from the HR system: effective last Friday.*

When delivering a Tier Two working number, name what has been verified and what has not.

Examples:

- *Cross-checked against the purchase order ledger for the largest commitments, which cover the bulk of the spend. The long tail is not yet matched to invoices.*
- *Reconciled against signed contracts for the major accounts. It does not include cancellations from the past week.*

When the business partner needs to choose give them the option explicitly. *This is directional. Let me know if you need the fully reconciled figure and I can have it by tomorrow morning.*

That last line is particularly important. It does not assume that the directional number is sufficient. It delivers the directional number because that is what the timeline allows and explicitly offers the definitive number as an alternative, with a clear timeline attached. The business partner now has all the information they need to make the right choice for their situation.

They almost always choose the directional number.

Because what they needed, in most cases, was never the fully reconciled figure. It was a number they could speak to confidently. And a number delivered with a clear, knowledgeable caveat is a number they can speak to confidently because they understand exactly what it is and what it is not

GETTING COMFORTABLE WITH AMBIGUITY

The deepest transformation that the Accuracy Dial produces in finance professionals is not faster delivery or better calibrated outputs. Those are the visible results. The deeper change is internal.

They get comfortable with ambiguity.

This sounds straightforward. It is not for finance professionals whose entire training has been oriented toward certainty toward the reconciled number, the closed period, the verified figure ambiguity is not just professionally uncomfortable. It is professionally threatening. It feels like the opposite of what they are supposed to be.

Getting comfortable with ambiguity does not mean getting comfortable with being wrong. It means developing the professional maturity to understand the difference between a number that is uncertain because it is poorly constructed and a number that is uncertain because the data available at this point in time has known limitations. And to communicate that difference clearly, confidently, and without apology.

The finance professional who has made that shift understands three things that most finance teams never develop explicitly.

- **How much time a given analysis deserves.** Not how much time it takes to reach one hundred percent accuracy. How much time it actually warrants given what the decision requires.
- **What level of accuracy is acceptable for different use cases and purposes.** The regulatory submission needs one hundred percent. The client conversation needs a clean directional number with a caveat. The internal strategic discussion needs something in between. The team knows the difference and applies it consistently.
- **That the discomfort of delivering an imperfect number is internal, and the value of delivering it in time is external.** The business partner does not feel the finance professional's discomfort. They feel the speed, the relevance, and the usefulness of an answer that arrived when it was needed.

That shift from managing their own discomfort to serving the decision is the moment a finance professional stops being a reporter of numbers and becomes a genuine business partner.

The next chapter addresses a question that naturally follows from the last two. You now know to ask why, who, and when before starting any analysis. You know how to calibrate the accuracy of the response to what the decision requires.

But what about the decisions your organization makes repeatedly, the same commercial questions, the same strategic reviews, the same

portfolio analyses that come around every quarter, every year, every time a certain type of decision needs to be made?

Chapter Eight introduces Decision Templates, the tool that turns the insight from the last two chapters into a permanent structural advantage rather than a habit that has to be rebuilt from scratch every time.

8

Decision Templates - Stop Starting from Scratch

The email arrived on a Tuesday morning, as it always did in the third week of the quarter.

A business development director at a professional services firm had identified a potential new client. A mid-sized manufacturing company looking for operational consulting support. Estimated contract value somewhere between £800,000 and £1.2 million over eighteen months. Could finance take a look and let her know if it was worth pursuing?

The FP&A manager who received the request knew exactly what was coming next. Not because he had a framework for answering it. Because he had answered this question before. Many times. And every time it arrived, it felt like the first time.

He opened a blank Excel file. He started pulling data on the firm's capacity, current utilization rates, available consultant hours, and the pipeline of existing commitments. He built a revenue model for the proposed engagement. He estimated the delivery costs. He calculated a margin. He stress tested it across three scenarios. He built a slide summarizing the findings.

It took four days.

On Friday afternoon he sent the analysis to the business development director. She replied within the hour.

The client had signed with a competitor on Thursday.

The decision had been made without finance's input not because the business development director did not want it, but because four days was longer than the window lasted. She needed a view on Tuesday. She had received one on Friday.

The FP&A manager filed the model in a folder on his desktop. He would never open it again. The next time a new client opportunity arrived three weeks later he opened a blank Excel file and started again.

THE REBUILD PROBLEM

There is a specific type of waste in finance that is almost universally overlooked because it is so deeply embedded in normal practice that it has stopped being visible.

It is the waste of rebuilding.

Every finance team faces a set of decisions that recur with predictable regularity. The new client questions. The project investment decision. The market entry analysis. The pricing review. The build versus buy assessment. These are not unusual or exceptional decisions. They are the normal commercial decisions that businesses make repeatedly as a matter of course.

And in most organizations, every single time one of these decisions arrives, the finance team that supports it starts from scratch.

Not because the decision is genuinely different each time. The inputs change with different clients, different projects and different markets. But the analytical framework underneath is identical. The questions that need to be answered are the same. The data that needs to be gathered follows the same structure. The output that the decision maker needs look the same regardless of what specific decision is being made.

The framework exists. It lives in the head of the FP&A manager who has answered this question seventeen times. It is encoded in the seventeen Excel files sitting in the folder on his desktop that nobody else can find, each one built slightly differently, each one using slightly different assumptions, each one reaching slightly different conclusions using slightly different methodologies.

Seventeen rounds of institutional learning. Completely inaccessible to anyone who was not personally involved in building each one.

This is the "rebuild" problem. And it costs finance teams and the businesses they serve far more than the hours of wasted effort suggest. Because the rebuild is not just inefficient. It is slow. And slow, as the previous chapters have established, has a cost that compounds every time a decision window closes before the analysis arrives.

WHAT A DECISION TEMPLATE ACTUALLY IS?

A Decision Template is a pre-built analytical framework for a decision an organization makes repeatedly.

Not a rigid model that forces every decision into the same shape regardless of context. Not a checklist that replaces thinking with process. Not a bureaucratic approval form dressed up as an analytical tool.

A live Excel model with three tabs, a clear structure, and a set of input cells that can be changed in minutes to reflect the specifics of the decision at hand that encodes the analytical framework the organization has developed through experience for answering a particular type of question.

The first time a Decision Template is built, it takes time. The framework has to be designed, the calculations have to be wired, the output has to be formatted. It is not faster than starting from scratch. It might be slower.

The second time it is used, it is roughly the same speed. The template exists but it is new and unfamiliar.

The third time, it is faster. The inputs are known. The structure is understood. The output is trusted because the organization has already seen it in action once.

The tenth time, the work that used to take four days takes one day.

The twentieth time, it takes a morning.

And something else happens by the twentieth time something more valuable than speed. The assumptions in the template have been refined by nineteen rounds of real outcomes. The revenue projections have been calibrated against actual results. The cost estimates have been adjusted by what delivery really costs rather than what it was estimated to cost. The confidence scores have been validated against the organization's real track record of execution.

The template has become institutional knowledge. The organization's accumulated understanding of what makes this type of decision succeed or fail, encoded in a model that anyone can pick up and use.

That is what seventeen Excel files in a folder on a desktop should have become. And did not, because nobody built the template.

THE ANATOMY OF A DECISION TEMPLATE

Every Decision Template, regardless of the decision type it serves, is built on the same three-tab structure in Excel.

The structure is simple enough that a finance professional can build it in an afternoon. Robust enough that it serves the organization for years. And clear enough that a non-finance business leader can read the output without needing the methodology explained to them.

TAB ONE: ASSUMPTIONS

The assumptions tab is where the decision lives. It is the only tab a non-finance user needs to interact with. Every variable that drives the analysis sits here, clearly labelled, in cells that can be changed without breaking anything else in the model.

For the recurring investment decision. Is this client, project, or investment worth it. The assumption inputs fall into three categories.

The first category is resources required.

- How much money?
- How many people, and at what seniority?
- What external resources like contractors, specialist skills, third party services?
- What marketing or business development investment is needed to capture the opportunity?

These inputs answer the most fundamental question a business asks before committing to anything: what does this actually cost us, in full, including the human capital that never appears on a budget line.

The second category is the return projection.

- What is the expected revenue? Over what timeframe.
- What are the key cost drivers that sit between revenue and margin.
- What KPIs does this decision impact beyond the direct financial return, customer numbers, market share, capability development, strategic positioning.
- And the headline financial outputs: ROI, NPV, payback period.

The third category is the one that most investment frameworks miss entirely, and the one that makes this template genuinely distinctive.

Confidence and clarity.

Confidence is the probability of execution. Not the probability that the financial projections are right. The probability that the organization can actually deliver what the projections assume. It is answered by two questions.

- Have we done this before?
- And do we have the people, systems, and organizational capability to execute at the level the model assumes?

A confidence score of 90% means the organization has a strong track record of delivering this type of initiative and the capability is clearly in place. A confidence score of 40% means the initiative is outside the organization's core experience, the capability is partially in place, and execution risk is significant.

Clarity is the roadmap score.

- Do we know, specifically, how to get from here to the projected outcome? Not in general terms in specific terms.
- Are the milestones defined?
- Are the owners named?
- Are the dependencies understood?
- Is the timeline realistic given everything else the organization is committed to?

A clarity score of 90% means there is a detailed, credible plan with named owners and realistic timelines. A clarity score of 40% means the destination is clear but the route is not. The organization knows what it wants to achieve but not reliably how to get there.

These two scores sit at the top of the assumptions tab, above the financial inputs, because they determine how much weight to give everything below them. A revenue projection of £2 million means something very different with a confidence score of 85% and a clarity score of 90% than it does with a confidence score of 35% and a clarity score of 40%.

The same NPV. Completely different decision.

This is the question that most investment appraisal frameworks skip. They model the return assuming execution. The Decision Template models the probability of execution and adjusts accordingly. The result is not just a faster analysis. It is a more honest one.

TAB TWO: THE MODEL

The model tab is where the calculations live. It is the engine room of the template. The place where the assumption inputs get translated into financial outputs through a set of calculations that the finance professional has built once and never needs to rebuild.

For most non-finance users, this tab is invisible. They do not need to see it, understand it, or interact with it. They change the assumptions on tab one and the outputs on tab three update automatically.

For the finance professional, this tab is the intellectual work of the template. It contains the revenue build. How the top line assumption translates into recognised revenue across the timeframe of the decision. The cost build, how the resource inputs translate into a full cost picture including the direct costs, the indirect costs, and the overhead allocations that projects always carry but estimates always understate. The margin calculation. The cash flow profile. The NPV and ROI calculations that feed the output tab.

The model tab is also where the confidence and clarity scores do their financial work. A well-built Decision Template applies the confidence score as a probability weighting to the projected return adjusting the expected NPV downward in proportion to execution risk. A £500,000 NPV with a 60% confidence score has an expected NPV of £300,000. The model makes that adjustment explicitly, so that the output reflects the risk-adjusted return rather than the best-case assumption.

This is basic expected value mathematics. Every finance professional learned it in their training. Almost none of them apply it to internal investment decisions, because the models they build from scratch never have a confidence input to apply it to.

The Decision Template does.

TAB THREE: THE OUTPUT

The output tab is the one page that goes to the decision maker. Not the workings. Not the methodology. Not the sensitivity analysis with seventeen scenarios. The answer.

It contains six elements.

1. **The decision summary.** One sentence describing what is being decided and what the recommendation is. Not a hedge. Not it depends. A clear, specific recommendation that the decision maker can act on or challenge.

2. **The resource requirement**, what these costs in full. Money, people, time, external resources. Presented as a total commitment, not a series of line items that individually seem manageable but collectively represent a significant organizational burden.

3. **The return projection**, revenue, margin, ROI, NPV. The financial case for doing it. Presented with the confidence weighting applied, so the decision maker sees the risk-adjusted return rather than the optimistic projection.

4. **The confidence and clarity scores presented visually**, as a simple indicator rather than a number. High, medium, or low. Green, amber, or red. The decision maker does not need a precise percentage. They need to know at a glance whether the organization is on solid ground or taking a significant execution risk.

5. **The KPI impact.** Which business metrics move if this works. Not just the financial ones. The strategic ones, the operational ones, the customer ones. This section answers the question that finance rarely addresses explicitly: what does success look like beyond the numbers.

6. **The roadmap summary.** Three to five bullet points describing the key milestones, owners, and dependencies. Not a full project plan. Enough to confirm that clarity exists and that the financial projections are grounded in a credible delivery plan.

That is the complete output. One page. Six elements. Everything a decision maker needs to make a well-informed call without asking a single follow up question.

THE REUSABLE FRAMEWORK MODEL

The best real-world illustration of a Decision Template working exactly as it should come not from a finance team but from an education technology company.

When one of the world's largest online learning platforms faces a recurring decision with predictable regularity. Should we launch this degree program? Different subject, different university partner, different target market but the same fundamental question every time. Is this worth doing?

At some point, someone built a template.

Feed in the assumptions, projected student enrolment, retention rate, tuition fee, delivery costs. The model does the work. Revenue projection, cost projection, margin, the financial case for launching or not launching.

What makes this example instructive is not the sophistication of the model. It is the assumptions it forces the decision maker to be explicit about.

Student enrollment is a projection. The template requires a number which means someone has to make a specific claim rather than a vague assertion about market opportunity. Retention rate is a confidence variable. How many students who enroll actually complete the program. This is the probability of execution applied to a specific metric. A program with high enrolment and low retention is not a successful program. The template makes that tension visible before the decision is made rather than after.

And here is what happens the tenth time the finance team uses that template. The retention rate assumption is not a guess anymore. It is calibrated against nine rounds of actual retention data across nine programs. The enrollment projection is not based on market research alone. It is informed by what nine previous launches actually delivered versus what was projected.

The template has become smarter with every use. Not because anyone sat down and redesigned it. Because real outcomes automatically refine the assumptions that future decisions are built on.

That is the compounding value of a Decision Template. The first time it is a framework. The tenth time it is institutional knowledge.

BUILDING YOUR FIRST TEMPLATE: MONDAY MORNING

There is no objection to Decision Templates that finance professionals make when the concept is explained to them. The logic is immediately obvious. The value is immediately clear.

The reason most finance teams have not built them is simpler and more honest than resistance. Nobody gave it a name. Nobody showed them what it looked like. Nobody said the recurring decision you have been rebuilding for five years could be a template you build once and improve forever.

Consider this moment.

Here is what Monday morning looks like.

Open Excel. Create three tabs. Name them Assumptions, Model, Output.

Before touching any of the tabs, answer one question. What is the recurring decision my organization makes most often that I rebuild from scratch every time. Not the most complex decision. The most frequent one. The one that arrives in my inbox and makes me think. Not this again.

For most finance professionals in commercial organizations that decision is some version of is this worth doing. A new client, a new project, a new investment, a new initiative. The inputs change. The framework does not.

On the Assumptions tab, create three sections. Label them Resources Required, Return Projection, and Confidence and Clarity. Under Resources Required, list every input that determines what this costs budget, headcount, external resource, timeline. Under Return

Projection, list every input that determines what this generates revenue, margin, key KPIs, strategic value. Under Confidence and Clarity, add two inputs a confidence score from one to ten representing the probability of execution, and a clarity score from one to ten representing the quality of the roadmap.

On the Model tab, wire every assumption input to a calculation. Revenue build, cost build, margin, cash flow, NPV, ROI. Apply the confidence score as a probability weighting to the NPV. This is the step most finance professionals will be tempted to skip because it feels uncomfortable to discount their own projection by an execution probability. Do not skip it. It is the most honest thing the model does.

On the Output tab, build the one-page summary. Decision summary, resource requirement, risk-adjusted return, confidence and clarity indicators, KPI impact, roadmap summary. Format it so a non-finance leader can read it in three minutes and make a decision.

The first time this template is used it will feel slower than starting from scratch. That is normal. The framework is being built alongside the analysis.

The second time it will feel roughly the same.

The third time it will feel faster.

By the tenth time, the work that used to take four days will take one morning.

And the business development director will receive her answer on Tuesday, not Friday.

The client will still be available.

CHANGES WHEN TEMPLATES EXIST

The transformation that Decision Templates produce is visible at two levels simultaneously. Inside the finance team and in the relationship between finance and the business.

Inside the finance team, the most immediate change is the one this example illustrates. The quality of the assumptions improves with every use. Not through deliberate effort but through the automatic feedback loop that a reused template creates. When the same model is used to project a decision and then the actual outcome is compared against the projection, the gap between the two becomes visible and specific. Which assumption was wrong. By how much. In which direction. That specificity is impossible when every model is built differently and filed separately. That is what turns a collection of historical analyses into institutional knowledge.

The second change inside the finance team is distributional. A Decision Template built by a senior FP&A professional can be operated by a junior one. The intellectual work of designing the framework has already been done. The junior professional's job is to gather the inputs and apply the judgement about what the assumptions should be, which is the part of the work that actually requires human thinking rather than spending their time rebuilding the infrastructure that the template already provides.

That frees senior finance professionals for the work that genuinely requires their seniority. Not building spreadsheets. Interrogating assumptions. Challenging projections. Advising on confidence and clarity scores based on organizational experience that a model cannot encode on its own.

In the relationship between finance and the business, the change is equally significant. The business development director who currently waits four days for a new client analysis will wait one day when the template exists. And the analysis she receives will be more consistent, more comparable, and more trustworthy because it uses the same framework as the last analysis and the one before that. She can compare this opportunity against previous ones not just intuitively but analytically, using the same metrics evaluated the same way.

That comparability, the ability to say this opportunity has a similar profile to the Henderson engagement which delivered 94% of its projected return, versus the Morrison project which had a similar NPV but a low clarity score and ultimately delivered 60% is something that rebuilt-from-scratch analyses can never provide.

It is the difference between a finance function that answers questions and a finance function that builds organizational intelligence.

There is a version of this that a CFO at an advertising agency built from necessity.

Every time a request for proposal arrived from a client, the same thing happened. The business development team needed a price. They had no framework for computing one. They went by instinct, by reference to previous retainers, by feel. The variation between proposals was wide. The time taken was inconsistent. And because finance had no template to point to, every significant bid eventually landed on the CFO's desk for a pricing sanity check that should not have required a CFO at all.

The CFO recognised the pattern. The business was not lacking the ability to price. It was lacking a reusable framework that made pricing consistent and fast enough to be done without finance in the room.

He built one. A simple template with four or five inputs, a ballpark retainer output, and a plus or minus ten percent band that defined the acceptable range. Below the floor or above the ceiling, the team came to finance. Within the band, they went ahead.

He trained the business development team to use it. Not as a finance tool passed down from above, but as their own instrument something they could run in the time it took to read an RFP, without waiting for a finance review that would add days to a process where speed was the competitive advantage.

The impact was immediate. Where the agency had previously taken several days to respond to bids assembling pricing, routing it through finance, waiting for approval. It could now turn around a proposal in hours. Competitors who were still routing every bid through their own finance teams were consistently slower. Clients noticed.

The CFO had not removed finance from the pricing process. He had removed finance from the routine pricing process; the eighty percent of bids that fell within normal parameters while keeping finance involved for the decisions that genuinely required it.

That distinction between the routine and the exceptional is what the Decision Template is designed to create. Not to bypass financial judgement. To reserve it for the moments when it is actually needed.

The next chapter addresses the moment that precedes all of this. The conversation between a finance professional and a business partner that happens before any analysis begins.

Decision Templates tell you how to build the analysis efficiently. The Stakeholder Contract tells you how to align on what the analysis needs to do before a single cell is opened. Together, they answer the question that finance teams most consistently fail to ask: what does the business actually need from us here, and have we agreed on that explicitly before we start?

9

The Stakeholder Contract

The meeting had been in the diary for three weeks.

A quarterly business review for the firm's largest retail client, a relationship worth £4.2 million annually that was up for renewal in six months. The commercial director had asked finance to prepare a full performance analysis. Revenue trend, margin evolution, cost to serve, year on year comparisons. Everything the leadership team would need to have an informed conversation about the relationship and what the renewal should look like.

The finance business partner had worked on it for four days. The analysis was thorough, well-structured, and accurate. Eighteen months of data. Clean charts. A clear narrative on the revenue trend.

The meeting lasted ninety minutes.

Forty of those ninety minutes were spent arguing about the numbers.

Not because the numbers were wrong. Because the commercial director's version of revenue, the contracted value of the relationship, which was how the sales team tracked it, was different from the finance team's version of revenue, the recognised revenue under the firm's accounting policy, which was how the management accounts reported it.

Both numbers were correct. Both were defensible. Neither had been defined before the analysis was built.

The leadership team left the meeting without making a decision about the renewal. A follow up was scheduled. The commercial director sent an email asking finance to rebuild the analysis using the sales team's revenue definition.

The finance business partner spent another two days rebuilding work that was already correct.

Six days of analytical effort. Zero decisions made. And a renewal conversation that needed to happen in a focused, confident ninety minutes had become a contested, unresolved discussion that would require at least one more meeting to complete.

The cost was not in the numbers. It was in the conversation that should have happened before the analysis began.

THE GAP NOBODY CLOSES

Chapter Six told you what to ask before starting. This chapter is about the conversation that follows. The one that determines exactly how to build what the decision needs

Every misalignment between finance and the business has the same root cause.

A conversation that did not happen.

Not a failure of capability. Not a lack of effort or commitment or analytical rigor. A specific, brief, practical conversation about definitions, sources, scope, and what a good answer actually looks like that both parties assumed was unnecessary and neither party initiated.

The finance professional assumed they understood what was needed. The business partner assumed finance would produce what was needed. Both assumptions felt reasonable. Neither was checked. And somewhere between the request and the delivery, the gap between what was asked and what was built became wide enough to derail a meeting, waste six days of effort, and delay a decision that the business needed to make.

This gap is not unusual. It is the norm. It happens in most finance teams, in most organizations, with most significant analyses. Not every time sometimes the assumptions happen to align and the output lands correctly without any explicit conversation. But often enough that the cumulative cost across a year of analytical work is significant, and consistent enough that the pattern should long ago have produced a standard practice for closing it.

It has not. Because finance culture does not have a practice of explicit upfront alignment. The request arrives and the work begins. The assumptions about what is needed, which definition, which source, which format, what level of precision, whether a recommendation is expected are made silently and individually rather than explicitly and jointly.

The Stakeholder Contract is the practice that changes this.

Not a formal document. Not a structured approval process. Not a bureaucratic addition to an already overburdened workflow. A brief, structured conversation five questions, ten minutes, before any significant analysis begins that closes the gap between what finance thinks it was asked to produce and what the business actually needs.

THE THREE MISALIGNMENTS

In the normal course of finance business partnering, misalignment between finance and the business takes three distinct forms. Understanding each one separately is important because each one has a different cause and a different solution and the Stakeholder Contract addresses all three simultaneously.

THE DEFINITION PROBLEM

The most common and the most damaging misalignment in meeting rooms everywhere.

Finance and the business are looking at the same metric and seeing different numbers. Not because either is wrong. Because they are using different definitions of the same word.

Revenue is the most frequent example. To a sales leader, revenue means contracted value, the total value of agreements signed, regardless of when the work will be delivered or recognised. To a finance professional, revenue means recognised revenue the portion of contracted value that meets the criteria for recognition under the relevant accounting standard in the current period. To a CEO, revenue sometimes means cash received the money that has actually arrived in the bank.

Three definitions. Three different numbers. All of them are defensible. All of them are correct by their own standard.

When a commercial director walks into a meeting with the sales team's contracted revenue figure and a finance business partner presents the management accounts recognised revenue figure, the gap between the two numbers can be significant. Not because anything has gone wrong, but because two different things are being measured using the same word.

The meeting that should be about the commercial decision becomes a meeting about which number is right. Which is the wrong meeting entirely. And it is a meeting that could have been prevented entirely by a single question asked before the analysis was built.

Which revenue definition should I use for this analysis: contracted value or recognised revenue?

One sentence. Asked before opening Excel. Eliminates the most common source of contested numbers in finance presentations.

Consider what happens in the weeks before a board meeting at a fast-growing B2B software company.

The CFO is preparing the investor update. One of the headline metrics is Net Revenue Retention (NRR). For the CFO, NRR has a precise definition: recurring revenue from existing customers at the end of the period, including expansions and upsells, divided by recurring revenue from those same customers at the start of the period. It measures how well the business grows within its existing customer base. The number her team produces is 108%.

The Chief Revenue Officer is preparing his section of the same board deck. He also has an NRR figure. His team calculates it slightly differently. They include revenue from new products sold to existing accounts by the new business team, not just the account management team. His number is 114%.

Both numbers are defensible. Both are calculated correctly by their own methodology. Neither team had explicitly agreed which methodology to use before building their respective sections of the board deck.

The board meeting opens. The CFO presents 108%. Fifteen minutes later the CRO presents 114%. A board member notices the discrepancy. The next twenty minutes are spent not discussing strategy, not debating investment priorities, not making the decisions the board meeting was called to make. They are spent explaining why the same metric produced two different numbers in the same presentation.

The board leaves uncertain about which number to trust. Both teams leave embarrassed. The CEO spends the following week managing the fallout.

Nobody had done anything wrong. Nobody had been careless or imprecise or unprofessional. Two capable teams had simply used different definitions of the same word. A word that appears in almost every B2B board presentation in the world, without ever checking whether their definitions aligned.

One question, asked three weeks earlier, would have prevented it entirely.

Which NRR methodology are we using for the board deck and is everyone working from the same definition?

The definition problem is not limited to revenue. It appears wherever finance and the business use the same language to mean different things.

- Margins, gross or net or contribution.
- Headcount permanent employees, or including contractors, or full-time equivalents.
- Costs, direct costs only, or fully loaded including overhead allocations.
- Customer count, active customers in the period, or total customers ever, or customers above a revenue threshold.

Every organization has its own version of these definitional gaps. Most of them have never been explicitly resolved. They sit beneath the surface of every financial conversation, producing confusion and contested numbers with a regularity that everyone experiences and nobody addresses systematically.

The Stakeholder Contract addresses them one analysis at a time. Not by resolving the organizational definitional ambiguity permanently. That is a longer project. But by agreeing, explicitly, which definition applies to this analysis, for this decision, for this audience.

THE SOURCE PROBLEM

The second misalignment type is closely related to the first but distinct enough to require its own solution.

Finance and the business are using the same definition but pulling from different systems. The number they are looking at has been calculated correctly in both cases. It is just calculated from data that sits at different points in the organization's data pipeline. And because data moves between systems on different schedules, the same metric pulled from different sources on the same day will produce different numbers.

- The finance team pulls revenue from the ERP, which reflects the fully posted, period-end position.
- The commercial team pulls revenue from the CRM, which reflects the live pipeline including deals that have been won but not yet posted.

- The data warehouse sits between them, refreshing overnight, capturing some but not all of the movements that have happened since the last refresh.

Three sources. Three correct numbers. All of them represent the same underlying reality at different points in the data pipeline.

When these three numbers appear in the same meeting. Which they do, regularly, whenever finance and commercial teams are both presenting to the CEO. The result is the same as the definition problem. The meeting becomes a reconciliation exercise rather than a decision conversation. Forty minutes spent explaining why the numbers are different rather than thirty minutes spent deciding what to do.

The solution is the same as the definition problem. Not resolved systemically at the moment of the meeting. Agreed explicitly before the analysis begins.

I will pull from the data warehouse for this analysis. Is that the right source or do you need it reconciled to the management accounts?

That question, asked before the work begins, means everyone in the room is looking at the same number from the same source. The reconciliation conversation never happens because the source was agreed before the analysis was built.

THE DECISION PROBLEM

The third misalignment is the least visible and the costliest. It does not produce an argument in a meeting. It produces something quieter and more insidious. A meeting that ends without a decision, a business partner who leaves without knowing what to do, and a finance function that has done excellent work and delivered no value.

It is the misalignment between what the business partner needed. A recommendation. And what finance delivered, an analysis.

In most finance teams, the standard deliverable is the analysis. The numbers, the trends, the scenarios, the sensitivities. Thorough, accurate, well-presented. And ending, almost invariably, with a conclusion section that summarizes what the analysis shows without stating what the organization should do about it.

The business partner reads it, understands it, and is no better equipped to make the decision than before the analysis arrived. Not because the work was bad. Because the work stopped one step short of the thing they actually needed.

Why does this happen so consistently across so many finance teams in so many organizations?

Three reasons. All of them are real. All of them compounding each other.

The first is fear. Having a recommendation means having a name on a decision. If the decision turns out to be wrong. If the analysis recommends proceeding and the project fails, if the numbers support the acquisition and the acquisition disappoints. The finance professional's recommendation is on record. The downside of being wrong is visible and attributable. The downside of not having a recommendation is invisible. The rational individual response, in a culture that punishes visible mistakes more than invisible omissions, is to present the analysis and let the business make the call.

The second is belief. A genuine, deeply held professional conviction that the decision belongs to the business leader and not to finance. That finance's job is to inform decisions, not make them. That having a strong view about what the organization should do is overstepping an intrusion into the commercial judgement that the business leader is paid to exercise.

This belief is not wrong exactly. The decision does belong to the business leader. Finance should not be making calls that are above their mandate or outside their expertise. But there is a significant difference between making the decision and having a view about what the decision should be. The business leader who asks finance for an analysis almost always wants both the numbers and the perspective of the person who spent four days building them. Delivering only the numbers is not respecting the boundary between finance and the business. It is leaving the most valuable part of the work undone.

The third reason is the most correctable and the most common. Nobody ever told the finance professional that a recommendation was expected.

Finance professionals who were explicitly told early in their careers, by a manager or mentor who understood what good finance business partnering looked like that their job was to have a view, not just produce analysis, almost always rise to that expectation. The expectation changes the behaviour. The behaviour changes the output. The output changes the relationship between finance and the business.

Most finance professionals were never told. They learned, through observation and feedback, that thorough analysis was what was valued. They inferred, from the culture they worked in, that the recommendation was someone else's job. And they delivered, throughout their careers, work that stopped one step short of the thing that would have made it genuinely useful.

The Stakeholder Contract does not solve this cultural problem permanently. But it solves it for each individual analysis by asking, explicitly, before the work begins, whether a recommendation is expected.

Five questions. Asked before opening Excel. Changes the output of the analysis entirely.

THE FIVE QUESTIONS

The Stakeholder Contract is five questions. Asked before any significant analysis begins. In a ten-minute conversation, a structured message, or a quick call. Whatever format fits the relationship and the urgency of the request.

They are not a formal process. They are not a checklist to be completed and filed. They are a conversation which can be natural, brief, and specifically designed to close the three misalignment types before they have a chance to develop.

QUESTION ONE: WHICH DEFINITION ARE WE USING?

For every key metric in this analysis, agree the definition upfront. Do not assume. Do not infer from context. Ask directly.

- *For the revenue figures. Should I use contracted value or recognised revenue?*
- *When you say margin. Are you looking for gross margin or contribution margin?*
- *Headcount. Permanent employees only or including contractors?*

The answer takes ten seconds to give. The alternative is discovering the definition was wrong after four days of analysis and takes two days to fix and forty minutes of meeting time to explain.

QUESTION TWO: WHICH SOURCE IS AUTHORITATIVE?

Agree the data source before the analysis is built.

- *I will pull from the data warehouse for this? Is that right? or do you need it reconciled to the management accounts?*
- *The CRM will have this as of yesterday. Is that close enough or do you need the ERP figure?*

This question does something beyond preventing the source conflict in the meeting. It signals to the business partner that the finance professional knows their data architecture which systems hold which numbers, at what point in the pipeline, with what known limitations. That signal builds confidence in the analysis before it has been built.

QUESTION THREE: WHAT WILL YOU DO DIFFERENTLY DEPEND ON WHAT I FIND?

This is the most important question in the Stakeholder Contract and the one most finance professionals have never asked.

It is not asking what data the business partner needs. It is asking what decision the analysis is serving. What will change if the numbers are positive versus negative. What action follows from what finding.

If the business partner cannot answer this question. If the analysis is exploratory rather than decision-serving, interesting rather than actionable. That is important to know before four days of work goes into producing it. Either the decision gets clarified, or the scope of the analysis gets adjusted to match the exploratory nature of the request.

If the business partner can answer it clearly. We will proceed with the renewal if the margin is above 18%, and we will renegotiate the terms if it is below 15%. The finance professional now knows exactly what the analysis needs to show and what level of precision matters around the critical thresholds.

QUESTION FOUR: DO YOU WANT A RECOMMENDATION OR JUST THE ANALYSIS?

Ask this explicitly. Every time. Without assuming the answer.

Most business partners want a recommendation. Most finance professionals assume they do not. Closing that gap in a single direct question eliminates the most common source of decision misalignment between finance and the business.

The business partner who says yes, I want your view gets an analysis that ends with a clear recommendation. The one who says no, just the numbers get an analysis that presents the findings neutrally and leaves the call to them. Both are valid. The difference is agreement rather than assumption.

And the finance professional who asks this question regularly is the one who makes it a standard part of how they initiate any significant piece of work and gradually establishes themselves as someone who has a view. Someone whose perspective is worth asking for. Someone who is a thinking partner rather than a reporting function.

That reputation, built one Stakeholder Contract conversation at a time, is the foundation of genuine business partnering.

QUESTION FIVE: WHAT ASSUMPTION, IF IT TURNED OUT TO BE WRONG, WOULD CHANGE EVERYTHING?

The final question is the one that focuses the analysis on what actually matters.

Every analysis is built on assumptions. Some of those assumptions are critical. If they are wrong, the recommendation changes. Some are peripheral. If they are wrong, the numbers move slightly but the conclusion stays the same. A finance professional who knows which assumptions are critical before they start building their analytical effort accordingly.

This question does two things simultaneously. It focuses the work on the assumptions that actually drive the decision which makes the analysis faster and sharper. And it gives the business partner a clear framework for challenging the recommendation when it arrives because they already know which assumption they would need to disagree with to reach a different conclusion.

It also surfaces, sometimes, a piece of information that changes the analysis entirely. The business partner who answers this question with actually, if the retention rate is below 70% this whole thing falls apart has just told the finance professional the single most important number to stress test. That information, shared before the analysis begins, is worth more than any sensitivity table built after it is complete.

THE SCRIPT

Same as every previous chapter. The concept needs a practical form that finance professionals can use immediately, without having to redesign it for their own context.

Here is what the Stakeholder Contract sounds like in practice. Not a formal document. A natural conversation opener. Sent as a message, asked at the start of a call, or raised in the corridor before the work begins.

Before I start, five quick questions to make sure I build exactly what you need.

1. ***First:*** *Which revenue definition should I use, contracted value or recognised revenue?*
2. ***Second:*** *I will pull from the data warehouse. Is that the right source? or do you need it reconciled to management accounts?*
3. ***Third:*** *What will you do differently depend on what I find? Are you making a go- or no-go decision or is this more exploratory?*
4. ***Fourth:*** *Do you want my recommendation or just the numbers?*
5. ***Fifth:*** *What assumption, if it turned out to be wrong, would change the whole picture?*

Five questions. Ten minutes. The analysis that follows will land correctly the first time because the brief was right before the work began.

The business partner who receives these questions will not think the finance professional is being difficult or over-cautious. They will think this person is serious about getting this right. That impression, formed before a single number has been produced, is the beginning of the trust that genuine business partnering requires.

WHAT THE CONTRACT PRODUCES

The Stakeholder Contract does not just prevent misalignment. It produces something more valuable a shared understanding of what the analysis is for, who it serves, and what a good outcome looks like, that both parties carry into the delivery and the decision.

The commercial director who answered the five questions before the quarterly business review analysis was built knows, when the analysis arrives, exactly what definition was used and why. She is not surprised by the recognised revenue figure because she agreed to it. She is not confused by the source because she confirmed it.

She does not need to ask what the analysis recommends because she requested a recommendation and one has been provided.

The meeting that previously spent forty minutes arguing about numbers spends ninety minutes making decisions. Not because the numbers changed. Because the conversation that should have happened before the analysis was built actually happened.

That is the value of the Stakeholder Contract. Not in the questions themselves individually they are simple, obvious, and take seconds to answer. In the habit of asking them. In the cultural shift that happens when a finance team makes explicit upfront alignment a standard part of how they work rather than an occasional practice of the most conscientious individuals.

The finance team that runs the Stakeholder Contract consistently does not just deliver better analyses. It changes the nature of its relationship with the business. Because the business learns, through repeated experience, that engaging with finance early before the work begins, not after it is delivered produces better outcomes than waiting for the finished product and hoping it lands correctly.

That shift from finance as a delivery function to finance as a thinking partner does not happen through a single conversation or a single analysis. It happens through the accumulation of fifty Stakeholder Contract conversations across a year. Fifty analyses that land correctly the first time. Fifty meetings that spend their time on decisions rather than reconciliation.

Fifty moments where the business partner thinks finance understood exactly what I needed before I fully understood it myself.

That is not analytical excellence. That is a genuine partnership.

The final chapter of Part Two addresses the moment after the Stakeholder Contract has been completed, the analysis has been built, and the finance professional is sitting down to communicate what they found.

Coming up next. Chapter Ten Communication for Action.

It makes the argument that even when everything else has gone right, the way finance presents its work can still slow the decision down, dilute the recommendation, or leave the business partner less equipped to act than the quality of the analysis deserved.

The chapter that follows is about making sure the last mile of the work is as strong as the first.

10

Communication for Action: Stop Presenting. Start Deciding

Most finance teams optimize for safety, not clarity.

More slides feel like more protection. More data feels like more rigor. More caveats feel like more honesty. The presentation that covers every angle, addresses every possible challenge, and documents every assumption feels, from the inside, like professional excellence.

From the outside it looks like a meeting that cannot make a decision.

This chapter is about the last mile of finance work. The moment when the analysis is complete, the recommendation has been formed, and the finance professional sits down to communicate what they found. Everything that came before this moment, asking why before starting, calibrating the accuracy dial, building the template, running the stakeholder contract can be done perfectly. And then undone in the forty minutes it takes to walk a leadership team through fifty slides that bury the answer somewhere around slide thirty-seven.

Communication for Action is not about presentation skills. It is not about making slides look better or speaking more confidently or telling a more compelling story. It is about a fundamental reorientation of what a finance presentation is for.

A finance presentation is not a documentation of analysis. It is a vehicle for a decision.

Those two purposes produce completely different outputs from identical underlying work. The documentation of analysis starts with methodology and works toward a conclusion. The vehicle for a decision starts with the conclusion and uses everything else to support it. Same numbers. Same recommendation. Completely different structure. Completely different impact.

The finance teams that consistently produce decisions rather than follow ups have understood this distinction. The ones that consistently produce requests for more analysis have not.

THE TWO FAILURES

There are two specific ways finance professionals undermine their own work at the moment of communication. They are not independent failures. They compound each other, and they share a single root cause. But naming them separately makes them easier to correct.

FAILURE ONE: THE FIFTY-SLIDE PROBLEM

The fifty-slide deck is the most visible symptom of finance communication that has been built for the analyst rather than the decision maker.

It is not built from incompetence. It is not built from a failure to understand what good communication looks like. It is built from a deeply rational, deeply human response to the professional environment finance operates in.

If the analysis is wrong. If the recommendation turns out to be incorrect, if an assumption is challenged and cannot be defended, if a number is questioned and the answer is not immediately available. The cost lands directly on the finance professional who produced the work. Visibly, attributably, with their name on it.

The fifty-slide deck is the solution to that risk. It is comprehensive enough that every possible challenge is pre-empted. It documents every assumption, addresses every scenario, covers every angle.

It is, in the most literal sense, a protection, a complete record of everything that was considered, built so that no challenge can find a gap.

The problem is that protection and clarity are opposites.

A presentation built to protect the analyst buries the answer inside the evidence. It forces the business leader to do the analytical work themselves. To read fifty slides, evaluate the methodology, weigh the scenarios, and form their own view about what the recommendation should be. The analyst has done the analysis. The business leader has to do the thinking.

That is precisely the wrong division of labor. The business leader's time is the most expensive resource in any organization. Asking them to extract a recommendation from fifty slides of documentation is asking them to do work that finance should already have done.

More slides do not make the analysis more credible. They make the recommendation harder to find. And a recommendation that is hard to find is a recommendation that does not get acted on.

FAILURE TWO: THE MISSING RECOMMENDATION

The second failure is the one that makes the first one so costly.

A fifty-slide deck that ends with a clear, confident recommendation is still recoverable. The business leader has worked hard to get there but at least they have arrived somewhere. The analysis that documents everything thoroughly and then stops. That presents the options, the scenarios, the sensitivities, and the trade-offs, and then concludes with something like based on the analysis the team would recommend further consideration of the available options has not just failed to communicate. It has failed to do the job.

Here is what a weak recommendation sounds like.

Based on assumptions A through D, we could consider Option 1 or Option 2, depending on market conditions and the board's risk appetite.

Both options have merit and the final decision will depend on strategic priorities.

That sentence is not a recommendation. It is a description of the analysis dressed up as a recommendation. It protects the analyst entirely. Nothing stated, nothing owned, nothing that can be wrong. And it leaves the CEO sitting across the table having just absorbed fifty slides of financial analysis with no clearer sense of what to do than before the presentation began.

The analyst has done the work. The CEO still has to make the call alone.

Here is what a strong recommendation sounds like.

We recommend Option 1. It improves cash flow by 18%, pays back in nine months, and the execution risk is manageable.

Here is why.

Six sentences of context follow. The recommendation is restated at the end.

That is it. A view, stated clearly, early, with the three numbers that matter and a direct acknowledgement that risk exists and has been considered. The business leader knows what finance thinks. They can agree, challenge, or ask for more. But they are engaging with a recommendation rather than assembling one from raw materials.

The difference between these two versions is not analytical. The underlying work is identical. The difference is whether the finance professional was willing to own a view.

Why do finance professionals so consistently produce the first version rather than the second?

Three reasons. All real. All compounding.

- **Fear.** Having a recommendation means having a name on a decision. If the recommendation turns out to be wrong. If the analysis says proceed and the project fails. The finance professional's view is on record. The professional cost of a wrong recommendation is visible and attributable. The professional cost of no recommendation is invisible. In a culture that punishes visible mistakes more than invisible omissions, the rational individual response is to present the analysis and let the business make the call.

- **Belief.** A genuine, deeply held conviction that the decision belongs to the business leader and not to finance. That finance's job is to inform decisions, not make them. This belief is not entirely wrong. The decision does belong to the business leader. But there is a significant difference between making the decision and having a view about what it should be. The business leader who commissions an analysis almost always wants both the numbers and the perspective of the person who spent four days building them. Delivering only the numbers is not respecting the boundary between finance and the business. It is leaving the most valuable part of the work undone.

Nobody ever said a recommendation was expected. The most correctable of the three. Finance professionals who are explicitly told early in their careers that their job is to have a view, not just produce analysis, almost always rise to that expectation. Most were never told. They learned through observation that thorough analysis was what was valued and inferred that the recommendation was someone else's job.

The Stakeholder Contract from the previous chapter closes this gap before the work begins. By agreeing upfront that a recommendation is expected. Communication for Action closes it at the moment of delivery by giving finance professionals the structure and the language to state a view clearly, early, and without apology.

▲ The Data Overload

The third failure compounds the first two. Even when the deck is a reasonable length and a recommendation exists, too much data and too many numbers bury the signal in noise.

The right number of core metrics in any finance presentation is three to seven. Enough to explain the decision. Not enough to recreate the data warehouse.

Beyond seven metrics, two things happen reliably. Cognition drops. The human brain cannot hold more than seven distinct pieces of information in working memory simultaneously, and above that threshold the audience stops processing and starts waiting for it to end. And discussion drifts. The meeting stops being about the decision and starts being about individual data points, each one generating its own question, its own tangent, its own request for clarification.

The finance professional who presents twenty-three metrics has not given the business leader more information to make a better decision. They have given them more information to get lost in.

The filter for what stays and what goes is a single question.

Does this number change the decision?

- If the number drives the recommendation. If a different value for this metric would produce a different recommendation, it stays.
- If the number materially affects the risk assessment if it tells the decision maker something important about what could go wrong, it stays.
- If the number answers the first obvious question an executive will ask when they see the recommendation, it stays.
- If the number is interesting but does not shift action. If it provides context or colour or additional depth without affecting the call, it goes to the appendix.

This filter requires a kind of intellectual discipline that finance culture rarely develops explicitly. The instinct, in a precision-oriented profession, is to include. Every number has a reason to be there. Every data point adds something. Leaving things out feels like incompleteness.

But incompleteness is not the risk. Irrelevance is.

The principle that governs every decision about what to include and what to cut is this: **relevance to the decision, not completeness of analysis.**

Those two standards produce completely different presentations from identical underlying work. **Completeness** says include everything that is true and accurate and related to the subject. **Relevance** says include everything that changes what the decision maker does next.

A complete presentation documents the analysis. A relevant presentation produces the decision.

THE SEVEN SLIDE STRUCTURE

If the fifty-slide deck is the problem, the solution is not thirty slides or twenty slides or even ten slides. The solution is a structure. A specific, sequenced, logic-driven framework that contains exactly what a business leader needs to make a well-informed decision and nothing else.

Every decision-driven finance presentation follows the same seven slide structure. Not because creativity is unwelcome or context does not matter. But because the logic of a good decision follows a predictable sequence regardless of what the decision is about. Decision, drivers, trade-offs, risk, action. That sequence works for a pricing decision, a market entry, a capital allocation, an acquisition, a cost reduction program. The inputs change. The structure does not.

SLIDE ONE: THE DECISION

The presentation opens with the recommendation. Not with context. Not with methodology. Not with a summary of what the analysis involved. With the answer.

We recommend Option 1.

Three to four supporting lines follow immediately.

- The quantified impact.
- What this does to the numbers that matter.

- One sentence on the primary risk acknowledged directly, not buried or minimized.
- The clear ask what decision is required from this room today.

This slide does something psychologically important before the presentation has properly begun. It tells the business leader where they are going. The rest of the presentation is not a journey toward a conclusion. It is the evidence for a conclusion that has already been stated. The business leader can evaluate each subsequent slide not as information to absorb but as support to assess. Do I agree with this logic? Does this evidence support the recommendation I was just given?

That is a fundamentally more engaged way to receive a presentation. And it produces a fundamentally different quality of discussion.

SLIDE TWO: WHY NOW

One slide of context. What changed that makes this decision necessary or timely. A performance gap, an emerging opportunity, a competitive threat, a market shift, a regulatory change. Something that explains why this analysis exists at this moment rather than three months ago or three months from now.

This slide does not need to be comprehensive. It needs to be honest. The business leader already knows the context. They commissioned the analysis. This slide confirms that finance understands the context too and has used it to frame the work correctly.

SLIDE THREE: THE ECONOMICS

Three to five numbers. The financial case for the recommendation in its simplest form.

Revenue impact. Margin impact. Cash flow profile. ROI. Payback period.

Not all five necessarily. The three or four that most directly support the recommendation for this specific decision. Presented clearly, with a brief label explaining what each one means and why it matters.

This is the slide where most finance presentations put everything they have. Twelve metrics, four scenarios, a sensitivity table, three charts. The discipline required to reduce the economic case to three to five numbers is significant. It requires the finance professional to have formed a clear view about which numbers matter most, which is itself a form of recommendation.

SLIDE FOUR: THE ALTERNATIVES

A brief, fair account of what was considered and why it was not recommended.

Not a comprehensive analysis of every option explored. Not a defense of the recommendation against every possible alternative. A clear, honest acknowledgment that other paths were considered, what they offered, and why they fall short of the recommended option.

This slide serves two purposes. It demonstrates that the recommendation was not the only option considered. That the analysis was genuine rather than a post-rationalization of a predetermined conclusion. And it pre-empts the most common challenge in any decision meeting: what about the alternative?

The business leader who asks what about Option 2 after seeing slide four knows that finance has already considered it and addressed it. The discussion moves faster because the obvious challenge has already been answered.

SLIDE FIVE: RISKS AND SENSITIVITIES

Two to three risks. Not a comprehensive risk register. The risks that could break the recommendation. The assumptions, if wrong, would change the call.

For each risk: what it is, what breaks if it materializes, and what mitigates it. Three lines per risk. Honest take about the downside without catastrophizing it.

This slide answers the question that every business leader asks, consciously or unconsciously, when they receive a strong recommendation: what am I not being told? Addressing the top risks directly naming them, quantifying them, and explaining what would need to go wrong for the recommendation to fail removes that suspicion entirely. The business leader who sees their top concern named and addressed on slide five trusts the recommendation more, not less.

SLIDE SIX: EXECUTION PLAN

What happens next? Who owns it? When?

Not a full project plan. Not a Gantt chart with forty dependencies. The three to five milestones that turn the recommendation into action, with a named owner for each one and a realistic timeline.

This slide does something that finance presentations almost never do. It connects the analysis to the operation. It shows that the recommendation is not just financially sound but operationally credible. That someone has thought about how this actually gets done, not just whether it should be done.

A recommendation without an execution plan is a recommendation that will be discussed, approved in principle, and then quietly forgotten as the organization moves on to the next priority. A recommendation with a clear next action, a named owner, and a specific date has somewhere to go.

SLIDE SEVEN: THE REINFORCEMENT

The presentation ends where it began. With the recommendation.

We recommend Option 1. It improves cash flow by 18%, pays back in nine months, and the execution risk is manageable.

The decision required from this room: approval to proceed to the next stage by the end of this week.

Restating the recommendation at the end is not repetition. It is architecture. The business leader who has just absorbed six slides of evidence hears the recommendation again with the full weight of that evidence behind it. The call to action: specific, time-bound, unambiguous which removes any remaining uncertainty about what this meeting is for.

The meeting ends. A decision has been made. Not a follow up. Not a request for more analysis. A decision.

THE APPENDIX PROBLEM

Every finance professional who has ever built a fifty-slide deck has heard the advice. Put the detail in the appendix. Most of them have followed it. And most of them have then walked through the appendix slide by slide during the presentation anyway.

Because the appendix, in most finance presentations, is not really an appendix. It is slides eight through fifty with a title slide in front of them. It gets presented just in case someone asks. It gets walked through because the finance professional built it and feels responsible for its contents. It gets shown because not showing it feels like hiding something.

And when the appendix gets presented, something specific and damaging happens to the meeting. It shifts from decision making back to analysis review. The room that was evaluating a recommendation becomes the room that is reviewing methodology. The business leader who was about to make a call is now listening to assumptions being explained. The momentum toward a decision built carefully through seven well-structured slides dissipates into the detail.

The right relationship between the seven slides and the appendix is not complicated but it requires discipline to maintain.

THE SEVEN SLIDES ARE THE MEETING. THE APPENDIX IS INSURANCE

The appendix opens only when a specific question demands proof, sensitivity, or detail that the seven slides did not provide. A board member who questions the revenue assumption gets directed to the revenue sensitivity in the appendix. A CFO who wants to understand the cost allocation methodology gets directed to the cost build in the appendix. The appendix answers questions. It does not get presented.

If no one asks, it stays closed.

This requires the finance professional to trust the seven slides. To believe that the recommendation is strong enough to stand without the methodology behind it being explained. That trust is hard to develop in a profession that has spent decades building its credibility through comprehensive documentation. But it is the trust that separates finance professionals who produce decisions from finance professionals who produce meetings about analysis.

When built correctly and when the appendix contains the full analytical work that supports the seven slides, organised clearly so any specific question can be answered immediately. It increases confidence rather than competing with the recommendation. The business leader who knows the appendix exists, who knows that every number on the seven slides can be traced back to a complete and rigorous analysis, trusts the recommendation more because the work is there if needed.

THE APPENDIX IS MOST POWERFUL WHEN IT IS NEVER OPENED

PUTTING IT TOGETHER

The five tools in Part Two of this book form a complete system. Not five independent practices that can be adopted in isolation in a sequence, each one building on the last.

1. **Always Ask Why** ensures the analysis is built for the right decision before any work begins.
2. **The Accuracy Dial** ensures the analysis is calibrated to what the decision requires rather than defaulting to one hundred percent precision regardless of context.
3. **Decision Templates** ensure the analytical framework is built once and improved over time rather than rebuilt from scratch every time the same question recurs.
4. **The Stakeholder Contract** ensures that definitions, sources, scope, and expectations are aligned before the work begins rather than contested after it is delivered. And
5. **Communication for Action** ensures that the work built correctly, calibrated correctly, aligned correctly actually produces the decision it was designed to support.

Each tool addresses a specific point in the analytical process where the precision trap typically reasserts itself. Together they cover the complete journey from the moment a request arrives to the moment a decision is made.

A finance team that has internalized all five does not just work faster. It works differently. Its relationship with the business is different. The conversations it has are different. The output produces lands differently. And the decisions it supports are faster, better informed, more confidently made. And these are different in ways that compound across every quarter, every year, every strategic cycle.

The business leader who works with a finance team that operates this way describes the experience in a specific way. Not that our finance team is very accurate. Not that our finance team produces excellent analysis.

They say our finance team makes us better at deciding. That is the job. Not the numbers. The decisions.

You now have five tools for escaping the precision trap.

A practical system for changing how finance teams work from the moment a request arrives to the moment a decision is made.

Part Three addresses the hardest part of everything that follows.

Not the tools. The change.

How to introduce these practices into a real organization, with real cultural resistance, real competing priorities, and real human beings who have been doing things a different way for their entire careers. ***The next chapter begins where every real transformation begins with a single conversation.***

11

How to Have the Conversation Your CEO Needs

The meeting had been in the diary for two weeks.

The CFO of a mid-sized consumer business had requested thirty minutes with her CEO.

No agenda shared, just a calendar invitation that said quarterly check-in. She had spent three days preparing for it. Not a deck. Not a model. Not a framework presentation about how finance was going to transform itself.

A single story. One concrete moment from the previous quarter that she had been thinking about since it happened.

Six weeks earlier the company had been evaluating a pricing change on its core product line. The commercial team needed a recommendation. Finance had built the model. A thorough, comprehensive analysis of the pricing elasticity, the competitive dynamics, the margin impact across twelve scenarios. It had taken three weeks.

The pricing decision had been made at the end of week one.

Not on instinct. Not carelessly. The commercial director had done a back of envelope calculation, discussed it with two senior managers who knew the market, and made a call that turned out to be directionally correct.

By the time the finance model arrived. Complete, rigorous, stress tested across every scenario. The price had already changed, the market had already responded, and the analysis was a historical document rather than a decision tool.

The CFO had filed it and said nothing at the time. But she had not forgotten it.

She walked into the CEO's office, sat down, and told him that story.

Not as a complaint. Not as a criticism of the commercial team for not waiting. As a pattern she had been observing for eighteen months and had finally found the language to describe.

"I think finance has been optimizing for the wrong thing,* she said. *We have been building for completeness when you need us to build for speed. And I think we can help you decide faster but we have to work differently."

The CEO put down his pen.

Good, he said. *What would that look like?*

THE CONVERSATION MOST CFOs NEVER HAVE

There is a conversation that needs to happen in most organizations between the finance leader and the CEO. It has never happened. Not because the finance leader does not know it needs to happen, but because the conditions for it have never felt quite right.

The conversation is not about strategy or structure or headcount or technology. It is about something more fundamental and more uncomfortable. The implicit contract between finance and the business about what finance is for.

In most organizations that contract has never been stated explicitly. It has been inherited. From the previous CFO, from industry norms, from the expectations that both parties brought to their roles without ever examining whether those expectations were actually serving the organization well.

The contract, as it typically operates, goes something like this.

Finance produces comprehensive, accurate analysis. The business uses that analysis to make decisions. Finance is accountable for the quality and accuracy of the analysis. The business is accountable for the decisions.

That contract sounds reasonable. It has a clean division of labour and a clear accountability structure. And it produces, in practice, exactly the dynamic that chapters one through five described. Finance teams that optimize for accuracy and comprehensiveness, business leaders who wait for analysis that arrives too late, and decisions that get made either without finance or in spite of it.

The conversation this chapter is about is the one that renegotiates that contract. Explicitly, specifically, and with enough concrete detail that both parties know what they are agreeing to and what they are asking of each other.

It is one of the most important conversations a finance leader will ever have. And most never have it.

HOW TO OPEN IT

The strongest CFOs do not open this conversation with theory.

They do not arrive with a framework about decision velocity or a presentation about analytical latency or a benchmarking study comparing their finance function against best practice peers. All of those things are intellectually defensible and all of them are wrong for this moment.

They open with a recent moment.

One concrete example: specific, recent, and chosen carefully. Where the way finance currently works costs the business something real. Not a catastrophic failure. Not a crisis that can be attributed to finance alone. A pattern, visible in a single story, that both parties will recognise as more than an isolated incident.

- The pricing model that arrived three weeks after the decision was made.

- The acquisition analysis took four days when the window lasted two.
- The market entry recommendation that was thorough, rigorous, and two months too late to influence anything.

The story is not a complaint. It is not an accusation. It is not an argument that finance has been doing its job badly. It is an honest observation that the job, as currently defined, is not quite the right job for what the business actually needs.

That distinction between doing the job badly and doing the wrong job is the most important thing to establish in the first two minutes of the conversation. The finance leader who opens with self-criticism creates defensiveness. The finance leader who opens with a pattern creates curiosity.

After the story, here is the one reframe. *I think finance can help you decide faster. But we have to work differently.*

Not that we need to be more strategic. Not that we need to be better business partners. Not that we need to upskill the team or invest in technology or restructure the function.

Those phrases have been said in every finance transformation program for two decades and they have produced, mostly, the same function with a new name.

This reframe is specific.

- Faster decisions.
- A different way of working.

Two things that a CEO can evaluate concretely rather than approve in principle and forget by the following week.

WHAT THE CEO SAYS BACK

When a CFO proposes working differently, sharper answers, earlier calls, directional recommendations rather than comprehensive models.

The CEO's reaction almost always surprises the finance leader.

It is not resistance. It is a relief.

James, the professional services CEO from Chapter Three, is not unusual. This pattern repeats across organizations and across industries.

Most CEOs do not want fifty slide decks. They tolerate them.

They have learned, through experience, that asking for something shorter or faster produces either

- A defensive explanation of why the analysis needs to be comprehensive or
- A reduced version that feels rushed and untrustworthy.

So, they accept what they get and work around it. Commissioning their own back of envelope calculations, relying on commercial instinct for the decisions that cannot wait, and quietly routing the fast, uncertain questions away from finance because experience has taught them that finance cannot answer those questions in the time available.

When a CFO says. I know you have been tolerating our process and I want to change it. The typical response is not skepticism. It is the question that signals genuine engagement.

Good. What would that look like?

That question is the opening. The CFO who has prepared for this moment knows exactly what to say next. The one who has not prepared tends to respond with something vague about being more agile or more responsive which produces a polite nod and no change.

Skepticism does appear, but in a specific form. The CEO who has been burned before. Who once accepted a rough answer that turned out to be wrong, whose board asked sharp questions that finance could not answer because the analysis was directional rather than definitive. Will push back on the idea that less rigorous analysis is better analysis.

That pushback is not wrong. It needs to be addressed directly rather than dismissed.

The answer is not that rough answers are better than rigorous ones. It is that calibrated answers, calibrated to what the decision requires, delivered in time to matter, with the confidence level named explicitly are better than comprehensive answers that arrive after the decision has been made.

The CFO is not asking the CEO to accept lower quality. They are asking them to redefine what quality means.

Quality is not accuracy. Quality is usefulness.

And a useful answer delivered on time is higher quality than a perfect answer delivered too late, regardless of how many slides it contains.

WHAT TO ACTUALLY ASK FOR

The CFO who walks out of this conversation with vague permission to work differently has not had the conversation. They have had a pleasant discussion that will produce no change because neither party made a specific commitment about what they would do differently.

The asks need to be concrete, behavioural, and time-bounded.

Three specific requests make the commitment real.

Request #1: Let us pilot this on one decision type for the next ninety days.

Not a wholesale transformation of how the finance function operates but a pilot test.

A contained experiment on a specific type of decision: pricing, commercial proposals, market entry, capital allocation. Where the new approach can be tested, evaluated, and refined before being extended more broadly. The pilot gives both parties a way to assess the change without betting the entire function on it. And it gives finance a specific context in which to demonstrate that faster, more calibrated analysis actually produces better decisions rather than riskier ones.

Request #2: When we give you a directional recommendation at seventy percent confidence, I need you to engage on the decision rather than ask for thirty more slides.

This is the behavioural commitment that makes the pilot meaningful.

The CFO is asking the CEO to change how they respond to directional analysis.

To treat it as a starting point for decision-making rather than a reason to request more work. Without this commitment, the pilot will fail.

Finance will deliver a directional recommendation. The CEO will ask for more detail. Finance will build more detail. The meeting will review the details. No decision will be made. And both parties will conclude that the new approach did not work. When what actually did not work was the CEO's response to it.

Request #3: If a call misses slightly, we treat it as calibration, not failure.

This is the most important request of the three. And the hardest for a CEO to make sincerely because it requires them to change how they respond in the specific moment when change is most difficult. When something has gone wrong and the instinct is to find out who is responsible.

The CFO who asks for this is asking for psychological air cover.

The explicit commitment that a directional recommendation that turns out to be imperfect will not be treated as evidence that the new approach does not work. But as data about which assumptions need to be refined.

Without this commitment, the culture change will not survive its first test. Finance will make a call. The call will be slightly wrong. The CEO will react with a question that sounds like why was this not modelled better. And every member of the finance team who witnessed that reaction will learn, instantly and indelibly, that precision keeps me safe and judgement gets me exposed.

The culture is decided at that moment.

Not in the conversation this chapter describes. In the first uncomfortable executive meeting where uncertainty shows up and the recommendation that finance made turns out to have been imperfect.

The CFO who has the conversation in this chapter is not changing the culture. They are creating the conditions under which the culture might change. If the CEO holds to their commitment when the first miss arrives, and if the finance leader responds to that miss the way the next chapter describes, the culture will change.

THE REAL ASK

Beneath the three specific requests is a single ask that is harder to make explicitly but more important than all of them.

The CFO is asking the CEO to become a partner in the change rather than a recipient of it.

Finance cannot escape the precision trap alone.

The trap is sustained not just by finance culture but by the CEO who asks sharp questions when a directional answer misses slightly and never asks sharp questions when a comprehensive answer arrives too late.

By the board that praises the thorough analysis without ever measuring what it cost in time. By the performance management system that rewards accuracy and never measures usefulness.

The finance leader who walks into the CEO's office with one story, one reframe, and three specific requests is doing something that most finance leaders never do.

They are telling the most powerful person in the organization that the problem is not entirely inside the finance function. And that solving it requires both of them to change.

That is not a comfortable message to deliver. It requires a level of confidence and a quality of relationship that not every CFO has with their CEO. It requires the finance leader to be willing to name a pattern that reflects imperfectly on both of them.

But it is the only conversation that produces real change. Because culture does not change when finance speaks differently.

It changes when the CEO responds differently.

The next chapter moves from the CEO relationship to the team. The conversation in this chapter creates the conditions for culture change at the organizational level.

Chapter Twelve describes what the finance leader does next inside their own team, in the day-to-day moments that determine whether the new contract with the CEO translates into a genuinely different way of working or remains a well-intentioned aspiration that the culture absorbs and neutralizes.

12

The Leader's Three Moves

The meeting started the way most internal finance meetings start.

A senior analyst was presenting the monthly commercial review. Twelve slides in she was still on the methodology. Explaining how the revenue variance had been calculated, which systems the data had been pulled from, how the adjustments had been made for the one-off items. The numbers were right. The process was sound. The explanation was thorough.

The finance director sitting at the head of the table had heard this kind of presentation hundreds of times. He knew what was coming. Three more slides of methodology, two slides of charts, and then on slide seventeen, the actual insight that the room needed.

He had two choices.

He could let it continue. The analyst had worked hard. The presentation was technically excellent. Interrupting felt unkind and the methodology would be finished in another four minutes anyway.

Or he could do the thing he had committed to doing every time this moment arrived.

He waited for the analyst to finish her current sentence. Then he asked one question.

Calmly. Without criticism. Without any suggestion that what had come before was wrong.

What is the decision this is pointing toward?

The analyst paused. She had not been asked that question before. Not in this meeting, not in any meeting she could remember. She looked at her slides, then back at the director.

I think, she said slowly, *that we need to reprice the Southern accounts. The margin is deteriorating faster than the forecast assumed and if we do not act before Q3 the recovery becomes significantly harder.*

The director nodded.

That is the presentation, he said. "*Start there next time...*"

Nothing else was said. The meeting continued. But something had shifted in the room that everyone present could feel and nobody could have articulated precisely.

The analyst finished her presentation. She did not forget that moment. In the following month her presentation opened with the insight on slide one. The methodology was in the appendix. The room made a decision in twenty minutes instead of fifty.

One question. Asked calmly. In public. Without blame.

That is how finance cultures change.

THE ANNOUNCEMENT THAT CHANGES NOTHING

Every finance transformation program begins the same way.

A finance leader newly appointed, or recently returned from a conference, or freshly convinced by a book or a framework or a conversation with a peer calls the team together. They share a vision. They explain why the function needs to evolve. They use words like strategic, value-adding, decision-focused, and business partner. They show a slide with a maturity model and a red circle around where the team currently sits and a green circle around where it needs to get to.

The team listens. Some are energized. Some are skeptical. Most are waiting to see what actually changes.

Then the finance leader goes back to their desk. The team goes back to their desks. The monthly close happens. The board pack gets prepared. The budget cycle begins. The fifty-slide deck gets built for the CEO review because that is what the CEO review has always required.

Six months later the maturity model slide is in a folder that nobody opens. The team is operating exactly as it was before the announcement. And the finance leader is wondering why the culture has not changed.

The answer is the same answer it always is.

Because announcing a change is not the same as making one. And in finance where the culture is not held in a document or a policy or an org chart but in the accumulated behaviour of every person in every meeting under every form of pressure the only thing that changes culture is behaviour. Specifically, the behaviour of the leader. Specifically, in the moments when the pressure is highest and the instinct to revert is strongest.

Culture does not shift with frameworks. It shifts when behaviour changes under real pressure.

There are three specific behaviours that distinguish the finance leaders who change their team's culture from the ones who announce the change and watch nothing happen. They are not complicated. They do not require a restructure or a training program or a new technology platform. They require consistency, courage, and the willingness to hold a different standard in the specific moments when the old standard reasserts itself.

THE FIRST BEHAVIOUR: MODEL BREVITY UNDER PRESSURE

The finance director in the opening scene did something that sounds simple and is genuinely difficult.

He interrupted a technically excellent presentation to ask what the decision was. Not in a one-to-one coaching conversation where the stakes were low and the audience was one. In a team meeting, in front of peers, in the middle of a presentation that the analyst had worked hard to prepare.

That is modelling brevity under pressure.

Not modelling brevity when it is easy and when the stakes are low, when the audience is receptive, when the presentation is already short. Under pressure. When the comprehensive methodology presentation is exactly what the culture expects and exactly what the analyst was trained to deliver.

The finance leaders who change their teams do this consistently. They ask what is the decision in executive meetings when their own team is presenting. They ask what would you do with this when a business partner requests an analysis. They ask what is the one number that matters when a team member walks in with twelve charts.

They do not ask these questions to embarrass or challenge. They ask them calmly, as a genuine inquiry, as the question that should always be asked and almost never is.

And they ask them publicly. That is the part that matters most.

A coaching conversation in private changes one person's behaviour in one context. A question asked in a team meeting changes the expectation for everyone in the room simultaneously. The analyst who hears their director ask what is the decision three times in three consecutive meetings learns, without being told explicitly, that starting with the decision is the standard. Not a preference. Not an aspiration. The standard.

The behaviour does not require a speech or an explanation or a reference to a framework. It requires the question. Asked consistently. In public. Every time the presentation drifts into methodology before insight.

That question "what is the decision" is the single most powerful cultural intervention available to a finance leader. It costs nothing. It takes ten seconds. And repeated consistently under real pressure it reshapes what the team believes good finance work looks like more effectively than any training program ever will.

THE SECOND BEHAVIOUR: REWARD JUDGEMENT NOT JUST ACCURACY

Finance performance management has a measurement problem.

It is very good at measuring what is easy to measure. Accuracy whether the numbers are right. Timeliness whether the deliverable arrived by the deadline. Completeness whether every section of the analysis was present and accounted for.

It is very poor at measuring what actually matters. Whether the analysis changed a decision. Whether the recommendation was clear and confident. Whether the finance professional showed the courage to state a view rather than hiding behind a range of scenarios.

The finance professional who produces a thorough, accurate, beautifully formatted analysis that arrives too late to matter and ends without a recommendation receives positive performance feedback in almost every organization. The work was good. The numbers were right. The deadline was met.

The finance professional who delivers a directional answer at seventy percent confidence in four hours, names the limitation clearly, states a recommendation, and turns out to be roughly right receives in most organizations no particular recognition.

And if they turn out to be slightly wrong, they receive something considerably worse than no recognition.

This asymmetry is the engine of the precision trap at the individual level. It makes precision rational and judgement risky. And it will not change until the finance leader changes it explicitly, visibly, in the specific moments when the choice between rewarding accuracy and rewarding judgement presents itself.

What does rewarding judgement actually look like in practice?

It looks like a finance leader who notices when a team member made a directional call that proved roughly right and says so publicly. Not in a general way about being more strategic. In a specific way about the specific moment.

You gave us a directional read on the Henderson margin on Tuesday morning. We made the pricing call on Tuesday afternoon. The full reconciliation came back on Thursday and you were within two percent. That is what good looks like.

That specific, public acknowledgement does more to change team behaviour than a values statement, a training session, or a restructured performance review framework. It tells every person who heard it what the new standard is. Not in theory. In the specific, named, praised behaviour of a specific colleague in a specific situation.

Rewarding judgement also means coaching the opposite behaviour without punishing it. When a team member hides behind analysis and when they produce a thorough presentation that documents every option and recommends none. The finance leader who wants to change the culture does not criticize the work. They ask a question.

What would you do if this were your decision?

That question does something the criticism never could. It puts the team member in the decision maker's position. It asks them to inhabit the role that finance is supposed to be supporting. And it reveals, most of the time, that the team member actually has a view, they have just never been asked to state it before.

The team member who is asked that question and answers it, for the first time, with a clear recommendation. And then sees their leader respond with interest rather than challenge has just had an experience that changes how they write every subsequent analysis.

Not because they were told to write differently. Because they were shown that having a view is safe.

THE THIRD BEHAVIOUR: ABSORB RISK UPWARD

Of the three behaviours this is the most powerful and the hardest to sustain.

It requires the finance leader to say, clearly and sincerely, to their team: if a call we make together turns out to be wrong, that is on me.

Not as a general statement of supportive leadership. As a specific commitment about a specific type of risk. The risk of being wrong in public, in front of the CEO or the board or the business leader who commissioned the analysis, about a recommendation that finance made.

Most finance leaders will say they support their team. Most will claim they do not blame individuals when things go wrong. Most will describe their leadership style as protective and empowering.

And then the first recommendation misses. The directional answer turns out to have been optimistic. The CEO asks a sharp question in a leadership meeting. The board requests an explanation.

In that moment that specific, pressured, uncomfortable moment the finance leader either absorbs the risk or deflects it.

They either say we made the best call with the data we had and here is what we are learning from it, or they say why was this not modelled more carefully.

The culture is decided in that sentence.

Not in the values statement. Not in the team offsite where everyone agreed that judgement was more important than coverage. Not in the performance review where speed and clarity were added to the assessment criteria. In the sentence that comes out of the leader's mouth in the first executive meeting where a finance recommendation turns out to have been imperfect.

If the sentence is we made the best call with the data we had, the team learns that making calls is safe. That being directional is supported. That the leader who asked them to stop writing for safety and start writing for action will stand behind them when the action turns out to be imperfect.

If the sentence is why this was not modelled more carefully, the team learns something else entirely. They learn that the announcement about judgement and speed was conditional. That the protection is available when the calls are right and withdrawn when they are wrong. That precision keeps them safe and judgement get them exposed.

And once that lesson is learned no framework can undo it.

This is why absorbing risk upward is the hardest of the three behaviours to sustain. It is easy to commit in a team meeting when no recommendation has been wrong yet. It is hard to honour in the executive meeting where a recommendation has been missed and the CEO is asking questions and the instinct to protect the function by explaining what the analyst missed is overwhelming.

The finance leaders who sustain this behaviour do so not because they are unusually courageous. They do so because they have prepared for that moment in advance. They have decided, before it arrives, what they will say when it comes. They have made the commitment to themselves and not just to their team. That the first miss will be treated as calibration not failure.

And when the moment arrives, they say what they prepared to say. Calmly. Specifically. Without drama.

We made the best call with the data we had. Here is what we are adjusting for next time.

That sentence repeated the first time, and the second time, and every subsequent time a recommendation misses is the most important sentence a finance leader will ever say. Because it is the sentence that tells the team, more clearly than any announcement or training program or performance review framework, that this culture has actually changed.

THE COMPOUND EFFECT

None of these three behaviours produces a culture change on its own.

One question asked in one meeting does not shift what a team believes.

One public recognition of a courageous call does not change how fifty analyses get written.

One absorbed risk does not permanently alter what the team is willing to put their name to.

What produces culture change is the compound effect of all three behaviours repeated consistently over time.

The team that has seen their leader ask what is the decision fifty times in twelve months has internalized the question. They ask this themselves before they start building. They ask it of each other in peer reviews. They ask business partners before accepting a brief.

The team that has seen three or four specific moments where directional judgement was publicly praised has recalibrated their understanding of what good work looks like. They have seen, through concrete examples, that the new standard is real and that it applies to them.

The team that has seen their leader absorb risk twice and actually absorb it, in real executive meetings where real recommendations are missed has made a fundamental update to their assessment of professional safety. They now know, from experience rather than promise, that making a call and being slightly wrong is survivable. That the protection is real.

These three things together, sustained over twelve months, produce something that no announcement ever could. A team that has stopped asking themselves how do I protect myself in this analysis and started asking what does this decision need.

That shift from self-protection to decision-service is the culture change that the precision trap requires.

It cannot be mandated. It cannot be trained. It cannot be installed through a new process or a new technology or a new org structure.

It can only be modelled. Rewarded. And protected.

By a leader who decided, before the hard moments arrived, what kind of finance team they were going to build.

The next chapter addresses a question that makes culture change sustainable in a way that leadership behaviour alone cannot. How do you know if it is working? The three behaviours in this chapter create the conditions for change.

Chapter Thirteen introduces the metrics that make that change visible. The feedback loops that the precision trap currently prevents and that decision-led finance teams need to build deliberately.

13

Measuring What Actually Matters

For three years the finance team at a professional services firm had been trying to change.

Not quietly. Visibly. With commitment. The finance director had read the right books, attended the right conferences, hired a business partnering specialist, restructured the team around commercial relationships rather than functional silos. He had done everything the transformation playbooks recommended.

And yet when he sat down with his CEO for the annual performance review of the finance function, the conversation felt identical to the one they had the year before. And the year before that.

The CEO was not dissatisfied exactly. The numbers were right. The reporting was clean. The team was responsive and professional and well-regarded across the business.

But when the finance director asked the question, he had been building toward for forty minutes. **"Do you feel like finance is helping you make better decisions?"**

The CEO paused for longer than was comfortable.

I think finance helps me feel more confident about decisions I have already made,* he finally said. *I am not sure it is helping me make them.

The finance director drove home that evening thinking about that sentence.

He had changed the structure. He had changed the language. He had changed the stated values and the team offsite themes and the job titles and the reporting lines.

He had not changed what he measured.

And what he measured: Accuracy, timeliness, completeness. This was telling his team, every quarter, every performance review, everyone to one, that the old standard was still the real standard. That the transformation was real in the announcements and unchanged in the accountability.

The next morning, he opened a blank spreadsheet.

He was going to build a different scorecard.

THE MEASUREMENT PROBLEM

Marcus had been a finance director for eleven years when he hired the best analyst he had ever worked with. Elena was exceptional. Her models were clean, her assumptions were documented, her variance analysis was airtight. In her first six months she closed the month faster than anyone on the team, caught three errors that would have embarrassed the function in front of the board, and produced a budget pack that the CFO described as the most comprehensive he had seen in a decade.

Her performance review was outstanding. Every metric the function tracked pointed in the same direction. Accuracy. Timeliness. Completeness. Elena was scoring at the top of every measure.

Eighteen months after she joined, Marcus had a conversation that stayed with him for years. He was having coffee with the chief commercial officer who was a direct, plainspoken leader who had been with the business for twelve years.

How are you finding Elena? Marcus asked.

She is very thorough, he said finally. Very accurate. I never have to check her numbers. I just wish she could tell me what to do. I get the analysis. I never get the recommendation. Last month I needed to know whether to pull the Hartley contract. I asked her for a view. She sent me fourteen slides. Beautiful slides. I still don't know what she thinks I should do.

Marcus drove home that evening thinking about his measurement system. Elena had optimized perfectly for every standard she had been given. Accuracy. Timeliness. Completeness. And she had done so, entirely rationally, by producing work that met those metrics precisely: thorough, defensible, comprehensive, and carefully free of any recommendation that could be challenged.

The measurement system had produced exactly the behaviour it was designed to produce. The problem was not Elena. The problem was that the measurement system had never once asked whether her work changed a decision.

Charles Goodhart, a British economist writing in 1975, identified this dynamic with a precision that has made his observation one of the most quoted laws in management: When a measure becomes a target, it ceases to be a good measure.

Finance teams know this law. They cite it in board presentations. They apply it to sales incentives, to operational KPIs, to every measurement system in the business they support. They have simply never applied it to themselves.

There is a principle in management that is simple enough to be a cliché and important enough that most organizations consistently fail to apply it.

What gets measured gets managed.

Finance teams know this better than anyone. They spend their working lives building the measurement systems that organizations use to manage their performance. They understand, at a technical level, that the metrics an organization tracks shape the behaviour of the people inside it.

- That measuring revenue without measuring margin produces revenue growth at the expense of profitability,
- That measuring customer acquisition without measuring retention produces growth that churns, that measuring activity without measuring outcome produces busyness without progress.

They apply this understanding rigorously to every part of the business they support.

They almost never apply it to themselves.

The typical finance function is measured on a set of metrics that were designed for a different version of the job.

- Accuracy of the close.
- Timeliness of reporting.
- Completeness of the budget pack.
- Variance between forecast and actual.

These metrics made sense when the finance function's primary purpose was to produce reliable financial information and they continue to make sense as a baseline of operational competence.

What they do not measure? What they have never measured? is whether the finance function is actually helping the business make better decisions.

That gap is not accidental. Measuring decision impact is harder than measuring reporting accuracy. The connection between a finance team's output and a business outcome is rarely direct or attributable in the way that a closed period or a budget variance is direct and attributable. And in an environment where precision culture already makes the finance team reluctant to own recommendations, creating metrics that hold them accountable for decision outcomes feels like a step too far.

But here is the consequence of not measuring it.

The finance team that is measured only on accuracy, timeliness, and completeness will optimize for accuracy, timeliness, and completeness. Not because they are not trying to be more useful. Because the measurement system is telling them, every quarter and every performance review, that usefulness is not what they are being held accountable for.

The Decision Velocity Scorecard changes that. Not by replacing the existing metrics. The close still needs to be accurate, the reporting still needs to be timely. But by adding a new set of measures that make the thing that matters visible for the first time.

THE FIVE METRICS THAT CHANGE EVERYTHING

The Decision Velocity Scorecard is built on five metrics. Each one measures a different dimension of what decision-led finance actually looks like in practice. Together they create the feedback loop that precision culture currently prevents the loop that connects the finance team's behaviour to the business outcomes that behaviour produces.

METRIC ONE: TIME TO USEFUL ANSWER (TUA)

Not the time to a complete answer. Time to a useful answer.

The distinction matters enormously.

A complete answer is the fully reconciled, comprehensively analysed, thoroughly documented output that finance teams currently optimize for. **A useful answer** is the output that arrives in time to influence the decision it was built to support.

These two things are not the same.

A complete answer delivered after the decision has been made has a time to useful answer of infinity. It was never useful, regardless of how complete it was. A directional answer delivered four hours after the request, with confidence level stated and source named, that changes the direction of a commercial decision has a time to useful answer of four hours.

Measuring time to a useful answer requires finance teams to track two things simultaneously.

1. **When the analysis was delivered and**
2. **Whether it arrived before or after the decision was made.**

That second piece of information is the one that most finance functions have never captured. They know when the work was delivered. They almost never know whether it was delivered in time to matter.

The first time a finance team measures this metric they will discover something uncomfortable. A meaningful percentage of their analytical output the exact number varies by organization but it is rarely below twenty percent and is often above forty arrives after the decision it was designed to support has already been made. The work was accurate. It was complete. It was delivered on time by every existing measure.

It was not useful.

That number whatever it turns out to be is the most important metric the finance team has ever produced about itself. It is the precise, specific, data-driven answer to the question the CEO was asking in the opening scene of this chapter. **Finance is helping me feel more confident about decisions I have already made.**

METRIC TWO: DECISION INFLUENCE RATE (DIR)

Of all the analyses the finance team produces in a given period, what percentage of them actually influenced a decision?

Not an informed decision but an influenced one. The distinction is between an analysis that a decision maker read and considered before making a call they would have made anyway, and an analysis that changed what the decision maker did.

The first adds confidence. The second adds value.

Measuring decision influence rate requires a brief, structured conversation with business partners after each significant analysis is delivered. Not a lengthy survey. Two questions.

1. **Did this analysis change what you decided or how you decided it?**
2. **And if yes, in what specific way?**

The answers to those two questions, tracked consistently across a quarter, produce a picture of finance's actual decision impact that no existing metric comes close to capturing. Finance teams that begin measuring this consistently discover that a surprisingly small percentage of their output changes anything.

The analyses that were most carefully built, most thoroughly documented, and most professionally presented are not always the ones that produced decisions. Often the most influential pieces of work were the fastest ones. **The directional read delivered before the meeting, the rough number sent on Slack before the call, the quick model built in two hours rather than two weeks.**

That discovery. That analytical speed often correlates more strongly with decision influence than analytical depth is the empirical proof of everything this book has argued. And it is only visible when you measure it.

METRIC THREE: RECOMMENDATION ADOPTION RATE

Of the analyses that included a clear recommendation, what percentage of those recommendations were adopted, challenged, or ignored?

This metric does two things simultaneously. It holds the finance team accountable for having recommendations; you cannot measure recommendation adoption if the analyses do not contain recommendations and it creates a feedback loop between the quality of finance's judgement and the decisions the business makes.

A high recommendation adoption rate is not, by itself, evidence that finance is doing its job well. A finance team that only makes recommendations when it is certain of the outcome will have a high adoption rate and very low decision influence because the recommendations will arrive for decisions that the business could have made without them. The metric needs to be read alongside decision influence rate to be meaningful.

But a low recommendation adoption rate is almost always evidence of one of two things. Either the recommendations are consistently wrong which is important to know and to address. Or the recommendations are not being taken seriously which is a relationship and trust problem that will not be solved by producing better analysis.

Both are problems worth measuring. Neither is currently visible in most finance functions.

METRIC FOUR: STAKEHOLDER SATISFACTION WITH DECISION SUPPORT

A simple, specific quarterly question asked of the business partners finance serves.

Not a general satisfaction survey about the finance function. One question about decision support specifically.

On the decisions you made last quarter that finance was involved in, how well did finance's input help you make a better decision? Rate one to ten.

Followed by one open question.

What would have made it more useful?

The score matters less than the trend. A finance team that scores six in quarter one and eight in quarter three has demonstrated something that no internal metric can show that the business partner's experience of working with finance has materially improved. And the open question, answered consistently over several quarters, identifies the specific gaps that the internal metrics might miss.

Finance teams that implement this metric almost always receive the same feedback in the first round. Faster. Clearer. Tell us what you think rather than just showing us the options.

That feedback is not a criticism of the team's capability. It is a description of the precision trap in the words of the people it affects most directly. And hearing it in those words from the business partners themselves rather than from a consultant or a book is often the most effective catalyst for genuine change.

METRIC FIVE: ANALYSIS REWORK RATE

Of the analyses delivered in a given period, what percentage required significant rework because they missed the brief, used the wrong definition, pulled from the wrong source, or were calibrated to the wrong level of depth?

This metric makes the cost of misalignment visible. Every rework is a Stakeholder Contract that was not run a definition not agreed, a source not confirmed, a scope not clarified. Tracking rework rate across a quarter tells the finance team exactly how much of their productive capacity is being consumed by work that was right the second time but wrong the first.

Most finance teams, when they first measure this, discover that rework consumes between fifteen and twenty-five percent of their total analytical effort. That number, one day in five spent rebuilding work that should have been right first time is the precise, quantifiable cost of not running the Stakeholder Contract before beginning significant analyses.

It is also a number that compounds powerfully when it is reduced. A team of five finance professionals that reduces rework rate from twenty percent to five percent has effectively added three quarters of a person to their productive capacity without any additional headcount. That is the return on investing ten minutes in a Stakeholder Contract conversation before beginning each significant piece of work.

BUILDING THE SCORECARD

The Decision Velocity Scorecard

Five metrics that make decision impact visible for the first time

METRIC	WHAT IT MEASURES	Q1 → Q2 ↑↓
01. Time to Useful Answer % analyses delivered before decision deadline	Not time to complete answer. Time to a useful answer. *Did it arrive in time to matter?*	63% → 81% ↑
02. Decision Influence Rate % analyses that actually changed a decision	Not informed. Influenced. Did the analysis change *what the business did?*	31% → 47% ↑
03. Recommendation Adoption Rate % of recommendations adopted by the business	Forces finance to have a view. Was the recommendation *trusted enough to act on?*	58% → 71% ↑
04. Stakeholder Satisfaction Quarterly rating from business partners	Did finance help you make a better decision? *Rated 1 to 10.*	6.2 → 8.1 ↑
05. Analysis Rework Rate % of analyses requiring significant rework	Every rework = a Stakeholder Contract that wasn't run. *Lower is better.*	22% → 9% ↓

Is finance helping us make better decisions —
or just making us feel better about decisions we've already made?

The Decision Velocity Scorecard brings these five metrics together into a single view that the finance leader reviews monthly and shares with the CEO quarterly.

It is not a replacement for the existing operational metrics: the close accuracy, the reporting timeliness, the budget variance. Those metrics continue to serve their purpose as measures of operational competence. The scorecard sits alongside them as a measure of decision impact.

The format is deliberately simple. Five metrics. Current quarter score. Previous quarter score. Trend arrow. One line of commentary on each.

1. **Time to Useful Answer:** What percentage of analyses delivered before the decision deadline this quarter versus last quarter.
2. **Decision Influence Rate:** What percentage of analyses changed a decision this quarter versus last quarter.
3. **Recommendation Adoption Rate:** What percentage of recommendations were adopted this quarter versus last quarter.
4. **Stakeholder Satisfaction:** Average score this quarter versus last quarter with one line on the most common feedback theme.
5. **Analysis Rework Rate:** What percentage of analyses required significant rework this quarter versus last quarter.

Five numbers. Five trends. Reviewed monthly. Shared quarterly with the CEO.

The first time this scorecard is presented to a CEO the reaction is almost always the same. Not surprise at the specific numbers. Though the numbers are often surprising. Surprise that nobody has measured this before. That finance teams have been running for decades without any systematic way of knowing whether their work is actually helping the business make better decisions.

That surprise and the conversation it generates is itself evidence that the culture is changing. A CEO who is asking what percentage of our analyses arrive in time to matter is a CEO who has made the shift from evaluating finance on output quality to evaluating it on decision impact.

That shift, reflected in a single quarterly conversation, changes what the finance team believes they are being held accountable for. Which changes what they optimize for. Which changes what they produce.

The measurement system becomes the culture change mechanism.

WHAT GETS MEASURED GETS MANAGED

The finance director from the opening of this chapter built his scorecard over a weekend. He presented it to his CEO at their next quarterly check-in alongside the existing operational metrics.

The CEO looked at the five new numbers for a long moment.

- **Time to Useful Answer:** Sixty-three percent of analyses delivered before the decision deadline.
- **Decision Influence Rate:** Thirty-one percent of analyses changed a decision.
- **Recommendation Adoption Rate:** Fifty-eight percent of recommendations adopted.
- **Stakeholder Satisfaction:** Six point two out of ten.
- **Analysis Rework Rate:** Twenty-two percent of analyses required significant rework.

The CEO looked up.

These are honest numbers, he said.

They are, the finance director said. *And they are going to improve.*

Four quarters later they had. Time to Useful Answer was at eighty-one percent. Decision Influence Rate at forty-seven percent. Recommendation Adoption Rate at seventy-one percent. Stakeholder Satisfaction at eight point one. Rework Rate at nine percent.

Not because the team had become dramatically more talented. Because for the first time they knew exactly what they were being measured on. Because the feedback loop that the precision trap had prevented for years had been created deliberately. Because the thing that mattered which is decision impact had been made visible.

And visible things, in organizations, get managed.

The next chapter looks forward. Finance teams that have built the culture, adopted the behaviours, and implemented the scorecard are asking a question that the broader profession has not yet answered

clearly. What does this function look like in a world where artificial intelligence is removing the manual work that currently occupies most of its time?

Chapter Fourteen argues that the answer depends entirely on whether the precision trap has been escaped. And that the finance teams that have made the shift from accuracy-first to decision-first are the ones that AI will amplify rather than replace.

14

The Finance Team of the Future

In 2019 a finance director at a logistics company had a team of eleven people.

Four of them spent the majority of their time on data gathering and consolidation. Pulling numbers from three separate systems, reconciling the differences, building the management accounts pack that went to the leadership team every month. It was careful, skilled work. It required people who understood the data architecture, knew where the gaps were, could explain the variances and trace every number back to its source.

By 2024 that work was being done in four hours by an automated pipeline that two of his remaining seven team members had built and maintained. The management accounts pack that had taken four people most of a month now arrived on the finance director's desk on the second working day of the following month, clean and reconciled, requiring only review rather than construction.

He had not reduced his headcount. He had redeployed it.

The four people who had spent their time gathering and consolidating data were now doing something different.

1. One was embedded with the commercial team, attending pipeline reviews and providing real-time financial perspective on deal structures.

2. One was running a Decision Template program building the reusable analytical frameworks for the twelve decision types the business faced most often.
3. One was leading the Stakeholder Contract process across the function, ensuring that every significant analysis began with an aligned brief.
4. One had moved into a newly created role of the decision analyst whose explicit purpose was to measure and improve the finance team's decision influence rate.

The finance director had not planned this transformation. He had responded to it. The automation had arrived and he had made a choice about what to do with the capacity it created.

He could have reduced headcount. The economics would have been straightforward.

He chose instead to answer a different question.

If my team no longer needs to spend its time gathering and reconciling data, what should it be spending its time on?

The answer to that question is what this chapter is about.

THE AUTOMATION IS ALREADY HERE

There is a version of the conversation about AI and finance that treats the disruption as future tense. A coming transformation. Something to prepare for. A shift that is approaching and needs to be planned for before it arrives.

That version of the conversation is approximately five years out of date.

The automation of routine finance work is not approaching. It is here.

It has been arriving, in waves, for the better part of a decade.

- Robotic process automation (RPA) eliminated the most repetitive transactional tasks first.

- Cloud-based ERP systems consolidated the data infrastructure that previously required teams of people to maintain.
- Business intelligence (BI) platforms put self-service reporting in the hands of business leaders who previously needed finance to pull every number for them.
- And now large language models (LLM's) and AI-powered analytics tools are beginning to do something that previous automation waves could not. They are starting to perform tasks that require not just processing but interpretation.

The finance function that is waiting for the AI disruption to arrive before deciding how to respond is already behind. The disruption is not a single event with a clear before and after. It is a continuous compression of the time and headcount required to perform tasks that finance teams have traditionally defined as their core work.

The question is not whether this compression will happen. It is what finance teams do with the capacity it creates.

And the answer to that question depends entirely on whether the precision trap has been escaped.

TWO FINANCE TEAMS, SAME TECHNOLOGY

Imagine two finance teams in the same industry, the same size, facing the same automation wave at the same moment.

1. Both teams have just implemented an AI-powered financial planning and analysis platform that automates variance analysis, generates first-draft management commentary, and produces scenario models in minutes rather than days.
2. Both teams have had roughly forty percent of their previous workload automated.
3. Both teams have the same decision to make about what to do with the capacity that has been created.

The first team is still operating inside the precision trap. Their culture rewards accuracy and completeness. Their performance metrics measure timeliness and correctness. Their finance professionals have been trained to build comprehensive analyses and present thorough documentation. Their relationship with the business is transactional. The business requests, finance produces, the business receives.

When forty percent of their workload is automated this team does one of two things.

1. They reduce headcount, because the work that justified the headcount no longer exists. Or
2. They fill the freed capacity with more of the same more comprehensive analyses, more thorough documentation, more scenarios, more backup slides. The technology makes it possible to produce more, so they produce more. The quality of the output, defined by the old standard of completeness and accuracy, improves. The decision impact, unmeasured and therefore unmanaged, stays the same.

THE SECOND TEAM HAS ESCAPED THE PRECISION TRAP

- Their culture rewards judgement and speed.
- Their performance metrics measure decision influence and stakeholder satisfaction. Their finance professionals have been trained to start with the decision, calibrate the accuracy to what the decision requires, and communicate for action rather than for coverage.
- Their relationship with the business is a partnership. They are embedded in commercial decisions, trusted with strategic questions, expected to have views.

When forty percent of their workload is automated this team makes a different choice. They redeploy the capacity toward the work that automation cannot do. The work that requires human judgement, contextual understanding, and the ability to sit across a table from a business leader and say based on everything I know about this business and this market and this decision, here is what I think you should do.

Same technology. Completely different outcome.

The difference is not the technology. It is the culture the technology lands in.

WHAT AUTOMATION CANNOT DO

Understanding what AI will do to finance requires being precise about what it cannot do. Not because the limitations are permanent. They may not be. But because the things AI currently cannot do well are exactly the things that decision-led finance teams have been developing as their core capabilities.

Automation is extraordinarily good at processing. Gathering data, reconciling numbers, identifying variances, generating standard commentary, building models from defined inputs, running scenarios across parameterized assumptions. These are tasks that require speed, accuracy, and consistency; qualities that machines possess in abundance and humans possess only with significant effort.

Automation is much less good at...

- Judgement.
- Understanding the organizational context that makes a financially attractive option operationally impossible.
- Reading the room in an executive meeting and knowing which number to lead with.
- Building the trust with a business partner that makes them willing to act on a recommendation before all the evidence is in.
- Absorbing risk upward when a call misses and maintaining the team's confidence that judgement is still valued.

These are not tasks that require processing. They require presence, relationship, experience, and the specifically human capacity to operate effectively in conditions of uncertainty without retreating into the safety of more analysis.

The finance professionals who have developed these capacities. The ones who have spent their careers building relationships, developing judgement, learning how to communicate for action rather than for coverage are the ones that AI will amplify rather than replace. The technology removes the processing burden that currently occupies most of their time and leaves them free to do the work that only humans can do.

The finance professionals who have spent their careers perfecting the processing. Those who have built their professional identity around the accuracy of the close, the completeness of the analysis, the thoroughness of the documentation are the ones who face the most significant disruption. Not because their skills are worthless. Because the skills that automation is best at replacing are precisely the skills that precision culture has spent decades developing and rewarding.

This is the deepest consequence of the precision trap. It has optimized finance professionals for the work that will be automated and underinvested in the capabilities that automation cannot replicate.

THE CAPABILITY SHIFT

The finance team of the future is not a smaller version of the finance team of today doing the same work more efficiently. It is a different team doing different work. The work that the precision trap has historically prevented finance from doing because the processing burden left no time or cultural space for anything else.

The shift is from four categories of traditional finance work to four categories of decision-led finance work.

From data gathering to insight generation. The time previously spent pulling numbers from systems and reconciling them becomes time spent asking what the numbers mean and what the organization should do about them. The finance professional who spent two days building the management accounts pack now spends those two days in commercial conversations, strategic discussions, and the specific human work of translating financial reality into business decisions.

From variance reporting to decision support. The monthly commentary that describes what happened becomes the forward-looking analysis that informs what to do next. The finance professional who wrote three paragraphs explaining why revenue was two percent below budget now writes the recommendation about what to change in the next quarter to close the gap.

From model building to assumption challenging. The time previously spent constructing the financial model becomes time spent interrogating the assumptions that drive it. The finance professional who built the acquisition model now spends their time asking the questions that determine whether the model's assumptions are credible. Whether the synergy estimates are realistic, whether the integration timeline is achievable, whether the confidence and clarity scores justify the projected return.

From analysis presentation to decision facilitation. The meeting that previously reviewed the analysis becomes the meeting that makes the decision. The finance professional who walked through fifty slides now facilitates a thirty-minute conversation that ends with a clear call and a named owner.

These four shifts do not require different people. They require the same people with the same analytical foundation doing their work differently oriented toward decisions rather than documentation, toward judgement rather than coverage, toward the business outcome rather than the analytical output.

THE WINDOW THAT IS OPEN NOW

There is a specific reason why the next three to five years represent the most important window in a generation for finance professionals who want to redefine what their function is for.

The automation is compressing the processing work faster than most finance functions are redeploying the capacity it creates. Which means there is a window. Not permanent, not unlimited, but real and open right now in which finance teams that make the choice to redeploy toward decision support can establish themselves as genuinely indispensable to the businesses they serve before the question of finance's value proposition is settled by default.

The finance teams that fill the automated capacity with more processing, more comprehensive models, more thorough documentation, more backup slides will find, in five years, that the additional processing is also automatable. That the floor keeps moving. That the work they have retreated into is no longer safe either.

The finance teams that fill the automated capacity with judgement, relationship, and decision support will find, in five years, that they have built something automation cannot replicate. Not because they are protected from technology. Because they have invested the time that technology created into the capabilities that technology makes more valuable rather than less.

The precision trap is not just a cultural problem. In the age of AI, it is an existential one. The finance function that continues to define its value through accuracy, completeness, and analytical thoroughness is defining its value through exactly the dimensions on which it will lose to automation.

The finance function that defines its value through decision impact, through the speed, clarity, and courage of its recommendations, through the quality of its relationships with business leaders, through the trust it has built by consistently telling the truth under pressure is defining its value through dimensions that automation amplifies rather than replaces.

The choice is available. The window is open.

The only question is whether the finance leaders reading this will make the choice before the window closes.

WHAT THE FINANCE DIRECTOR DID?

The finance director from the opening of this chapter made his choice in 2024 without knowing it was a window. He made it because the automation arrived and he asked himself an honest question about what his team should be doing with the capacity it created.

Four years later his team of seven is regarded, across the business, as the function that makes decisions better. Not the function that reports accurately. Not the function that produces thorough analysis. The function that arrives with a view, states it clearly, and stands behind it when the pressure is on.

His CEO describes working with the finance team in a specific way.

Not they give us great analysis. Not they are accurate and reliable.

She says when finance is in the room, we make better decisions.

That is the job. Not the numbers. Not the models. Not the slides.

The decisions.

And it has always been the job. The precision trap just made it invisible.

The final chapter is a letter. Not a framework. Not a case study. Not a set of tools or metrics or behavioural commitments.

A direct communication from one finance professional to another about what this work is really for, why escaping the trap is worth the discomfort it requires, and what becomes possible on the other side. It is the chapter that was always underneath the book.

15

The Choice

If you have read fourteen chapters of this book and you are still here, you already know.

You have recognised yourself somewhere in these pages.

Not as a villain. Not as someone incompetent. Not as someone who doesn't care.

But as someone who has been trained. Very well trained to optimize for something that is no longer the scarcest resource in the room.

And now you are sitting with a quiet question:

Am I willing to change how I work?

Let me speak to you directly.

Not as an author.

Not as someone trying to win an argument.

But as someone who has sat exactly where you are sitting.

WHAT I MOST WANT YOU TO KNOW

You are not paid to be right.

You are paid to be useful.

Those two things overlap sometimes. But they are not the same.

The most valuable finance professionals I have worked with

- They were not the ones who could build the most complex models.
- They were not the ones who caught every rounding error.
- They were not the ones whose decks were technically flawless.

They were the ones who could walk into a room where a decision was forming and shape it.

- They were early.
- They were clear.
- They were willing to own a view.

And they understood something most finance professionals never consciously articulate:

The business does not experience you as an analyst. It experiences you as latency or leverage.

You are either speeding up good decisions. Or slowing them down.

There is no neutral position.

WHAT I WISH SOMEONE HAD TOLD ME

I wish someone had told me earlier that perfection is often fear in disguise.

Fear of being wrong.

Fear of being challenged.

Fear of having your name attached to a decision that fails.

Finance culture rewards defensibility. It quietly penalizes exposure. So, we learn to protect ourselves with comprehensiveness. With caveats. With scenarios. With fifty slides instead of five.

It feels professional.

But here is the truth that I learned slowly and painfully:

No CEO ever said, "I wish finance had taken two more weeks."

They say:

- "I wish we had moved faster."
- "I wish we had known that earlier."
- "Why didn't finance raise this before?"

The cost of being wrong once is visible.

The cost of being late repeatedly is invisible.

And because it is invisible, it compounds.

I wish someone had told me that the real risk in finance is not being wrong. It is being irrelevant.

THE COST OF STAYING INSIDE THE TRAP

I have seen three costs most clearly.

1. **You Get Invited Later**

When you consistently arrive after decisions are already forming, something subtle happens.

Leaders stop waiting.

They don't fire you.

They don't criticize you.

They don't even tell you.

They just start making early calls without you.

Finance becomes the validation function instead of the shaping function.

You still build excellent analysis.

You just build it around decisions that are already emotionally committed.

And that is the beginning of marginalization.

Not dramatic.

Not political.

Just quiet irrelevance.

2. **You Burn Energy on Insurance Instead of Impact**

I have worked with teams where 30% of their effort went into protection.

Extra reconciliations that didn't change the recommendation.

Sensitivity tables no one used.

Appendix slides that were never opened.

Brilliant people spend their cognitive energy defending themselves against hypothetical challenges instead of pushing the business forward.

They were exhausted.

Not because they lacked capability.

Because they were misallocating it.

When you operate inside the trap, you confuse effort with value.

And over time, that erodes motivation.

3. **You Cap Your Own Influence**

This is the hardest one to admit.

The finance professionals who stay inside the trap often plateau.

Not because they are not intelligent.

Not because they are not hardworking.

But because influence in senior roles is built on judgement under uncertainty.

If you need 95% certainty before you speak clearly, you will never be the voice in the room when it matters most. The moments that shape careers and companies rarely arrive fully modelled.

They arrive messy.

Time-constrained.

Incomplete.

If you cannot operate there, someone else will.

THE REAL QUESTION

This is not about abandoning rigor.

This is not about guessing.

This is not about lowering standards.

It is about recalibrating.

About asking, before you open Excel:

- What decision is this for?
- When does it need to land?
- How accurate does it actually need to be to change the direction?

It is about being willing to deliver a 70% answer when 70% is enough.

It is about being explicit about confidence levels instead of hiding behind completeness.

It is about saying:

"Here is our recommendation. Here is why. Here is the risk. And this is good enough to act."

That sentence will feel uncomfortable the first few times you say it.

Say it anyway.

If You Change. If you make this shift, three things happen.

1. You get pulled earlier into conversations.
2. You spend less time rebuilding work. And
3. You start to feel something many finance professionals have quietly lost: Momentum.

Decisions move.

You see the impact.

You see outcomes connected to your input.

Finance becomes alive again.

THE FINAL CHOICE

The precision trap is not enforced by your CEO.

It is not mandated by your ERP system.

It is not written into your job description.

It is sustained by habit.

And habits can be changed.

But here is the honest part.

Changing how you work will make you uncomfortable before it makes you effective.

You will feel exposed.

You will feel like you are cutting corners.

You will feel like you are speaking too early.

That feeling is not incompetence.

It is growth.

If I could sit across from you right now, after fourteen chapters, this is what I would say:

You did not become a finance professional to reconcile spreadsheets.

You became one to influence decisions.

Do not let your training become your ceiling.

Be the person who brings clarity before the window closes.

Be the person who owns a view.

Be the person who is useful when it matters.

Because the most expensive answer in the room is not the wrong one.

It is the one that arrives too late. And you are capable of being earlier.

CONCLUSION

The argument this book has made is a simple one.

Modern finance functions are optimizing for analytical perfection in a world where decision speed and clarity create more value than incremental accuracy. That misalignment between what finance measures itself on and what organizations actually need from it quietly costs businesses influence, opportunity, and relevance. Not through dramatic failure. Through the accumulated weight of analyses that arrived too late, recommendations that were never made, and decisions that moved without finance because finance was not ready.

The precision trap is not a recent development. It has been building for decades, reinforced by every accounting qualification that rewarded accuracy over usefulness, every performance review that measured completeness over impact, every executive meeting that tolerated the fifty-slide deck without ever asking what it cost in the decision that did not wait.

It is invisible from inside because it looks exactly like professionalism. The thorough analysis. The complete reconciliation. The airtight model. These things are not wrong. They are necessary. The trap is not in doing them. It is in doing only them in allowing the standard of analytical completeness to crowd out the standard of decision usefulness, and in never noticing that the two standards are not the same thing.

This book has given you five tools for escaping the trap. A way of asking why before starting. A framework for calibrating the accuracy dial to what decisions actually require. A system for building analytical frameworks that compound in value rather than starting from scratch every time. A practice for aligning with business partners before the work begins. And a structure for communicating in a way that produces decisions rather than discussions.

These tools work. But they are not the point.

The point is the orientation underneath them.

Walk into every request, every model, every meeting with one governing question.

Will this help the decision move forward in time?

Not, is this analysis complete. Not, have I covered every scenario. Not, can I defend every assumption if challenged.

Will this help the decision move forward in time?

That question, asked honestly before every piece of work begins, makes the tools obvious and the trade-offs clear. It tells you when the directional answer is enough and when the full reconciliation is necessary. It tells you when to send the slack / teams message and when the brief is already clear. It tells you when seven slides are the right format and when the appendix should stay closed.

It tells you, above all, what finance was always meant to be.

Not the function that validates decisions after they are formed. Not the checkpoint that slows the organization down while it perfects the analysis. Not the room that gets consulted after the direction has already been set.

The function that shapes decisions while they are still fluid. That arrives early enough to matter. That states a view clearly enough to be useful. That stands behind its recommendations under pressure and learns from the ones that miss.

A catalyst. Not a checkpoint.

That is the job. It has always been the job.

The precision trap just made it easy to forget.

About the Author

Asif Masani is a Chartered Accountant, author, and an educator on a mission to help one million finance professionals master Finance, AI and FP&A skills.

He is the founder of FP&A Professionals Institute (FPI). He is also the Program Director of the CGFPA® certification. The CGFPA® is one of the few globally recognised credentials dedicated exclusively to Financial Planning and Analysis. Its community spans more than a hundred countries.

Before building FPI full time, Asif spent over a decade in corporate finance. He began his career as an auditor at EY before moving into FP&A at Citi. He progressed from FP&A Analyst to FP&A Manager and ultimately to FP&A Lead for the APAC region at one of the world's largest EdTech companies. He made the transition to full time education and institution building in 2023.

He is the author of All About FP&A, From Accounting to FP&A, and The Data Storytelling Playbook. All three have been read by finance professionals across the globe. The Precision Trap is his fourth book.

Asif creates finance, FP&A and AI education content for over 150,000 followers across LinkedIn and YouTube. He writes and speaks about FP&A, business partnering, AI in finance, and the evolving role of the modern finance professional.

To learn more about Asif's work, the CGFPA® certification, and the FP&A Professionals Institute, visit: www.fpnaprofessionals.com

Also by the Author

All About FP&A: A comprehensive guide to Financial Planning and Analysis for finance professionals looking to understand the full scope of the FP&A function. Covers forecasting, budgeting, variance analysis, business partnering, and the tools and mindset required to excel in modern FP&A roles.

From Accounting to FP&A: A practical roadmap for accounting and finance professionals making the transition into FP&A. Covers the mindset shift required, the skills to develop, the roles available, and the strategies that accelerate the journey from technical accountant to strategic finance business partner.

The Data Storytelling Playbook: A practical guide to communicating financial data with clarity and impact. Covers how to structure financial narratives, build compelling visualisations, and present numbers in a way that drives decisions rather than documents them.

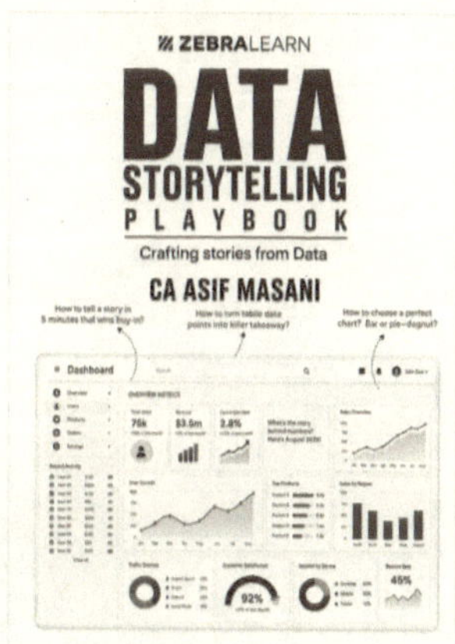

All titles are available on Amazon worldwide.

To explore these titles and other resources from FP&A Professionals Institute, visit:

www.fpnaprofessionals.com

Key Concepts - Bibliography

The Precision Trap: The cultural tendency of finance teams to optimise for accuracy and completeness at the expense of speed and usefulness. The trap is invisible from the inside because it looks exactly like professionalism.

Analytical Latency: The time between a decision becoming available and a finance team delivering analysis that could influence it. The hidden cost that never appears in any variance report.

The Time Value of Decisions: The principle that the value of an analysis decays over time. A 70% accurate answer delivered on Day 1 creates more value than a 100% accurate answer delivered on Day 10, regardless of how many slides it contains.

Decision Tiering: The practice of classifying a decision by urgency, audience and reversibility before beginning any analysis. The three questions: Why, Who and When determine which tier of analysis the decision requires.

The Accuracy Dial: The framework for calibrating analytical precision to what a decision actually requires rather than defaulting to the highest standard regardless of context. The dial has three settings: Directional, Working, and Definitive.

Tier 1. Directional Number: An analysis produced in minutes from the most accessible authoritative source. Named source, stated limitation, no reconciliation. Appropriate for client conversations, quick internal questions, and go or no-go decisions.

Tier 2. Working Number: An analysis produced in hours. Cross-checked against a second source for the key items that drive the majority of value. Appropriate for leadership reviews, commercial proposals, and internal strategic discussions.

Tier 3. Definitive Number: A fully reconciled analysis with a complete audit trail. Every line verified and defensible under external scrutiny. Appropriate for board decisions, regulatory submissions, statutory accounts, and acquisition analysis.

The Stakeholder Contract: The five-question pre-analysis brief completed before beginning any significant piece of work. Covers definition, source, decision, recommendation, and format. Prevents the most common causes of rework.

Time to Useful Answer (TUA): The time between a request arriving and a useful answer being delivered. Not the time to a complete answer. The metric that measures whether analysis arrived in time to matter.

Decision Influence Rate (DIR): The percentage of analyses produced by a finance team that actually changed a decision. Not analyses that informed a decision. Analyses that influenced it. The most honest measure of finance's impact on the business.

Recommendation Adoption Rate (RAR): The percentage of analyses that included a clear recommendation where that recommendation was adopted by the business. Holds finance accountable for having a view, not just presenting data.

Analysis Rework Rate (ARR): The percentage of analyses that required significant rework because they missed the brief, used the wrong definition, or were calibrated to the wrong level of depth. Every rework is a Stakeholder Contract that was not run.

The Competence Paradox: The observation that the most skilled finance professionals are often the most deeply embedded in the precision trap. Skill provides the capability to build more comprehensive analyses. Judgement is required to know when not to.

The Missing Feedback Loop: The structural absence of any mechanism that connects analytical latency to business outcomes. Finance teams receive feedback on accuracy and timeliness but almost never receive feedback on whether their analysis arrived in time to change anything.

The Decision Velocity Scorecard: The five-metric framework for measuring finance's decision impact. Comprises Time to Useful Answer, Decision Influence Rate, Recommendation Adoption Rate, Stakeholder Satisfaction, and Analysis Rework Rate.

Absorbing Risk Upward: The leadership behaviour of taking responsibility when a directional recommendation turns out to be imperfect rather than deflecting accountability to the analyst. The behaviour that signals to a finance team that making calls is safe.

The Precision Trap Pipeline: The six-stage cycle through which precision culture reproduces itself. Training, First Job, Feedback, Identity, Incentives, and Culture. Each stage reinforces the next, creating a self-perpetuating system that is difficult to break without deliberate intervention.

Decision-Led Finance: The orientation of a finance team around decision impact rather than analytical accuracy. The alternative to the precision trap. Characterised by speed, judgement, clear recommendations, and metrics that measure usefulness rather than completeness.

The Body Set Weight Analogy: The comparison between precision culture and the body's internal thermostat. Just as cutting calories fails when the thermostat is set too high, telling a finance team to move faster fails when the culture is calibrated to precision. The thermostat must be reset, not fought.

Free Companion Workbook

The frameworks and tools in this book are designed to be used, not just read.

To make that easier, a free companion workbook has been created to go alongside The Precision Trap. It contains eight practical templates, one for each of the book's core tools, built in Excel and ready to use from your first working day after finishing this book.

What is inside:

1. The Decision Tiering Log. Log every analysis request through the three questions before opening Excel.
2. The Accuracy Dial Tracker. Track the tier you chose against the tier you would have defaulted to, and measure the time saved.
3. The Stakeholder Contract. A five-question pre-analysis brief to complete before beginning any significant piece of work.
4. The Communication Planner. A seven-slide structure template for any finance presentation designed to produce a decision, not a discussion.
5. The CEO Conversation Prep. A structured preparation sheet for the conversation that renegotiates the implicit contract between finance and the business.
6. The Culture Change Tracker. Log the three leadership behaviours that shift finance culture over time.

7. The Decision Velocity Scorecard. A live quarterly scorecard with the five metrics that make decision impact visible for the first time.
8. The Analysis Pipeline. A master log of all analyses in progress, tracking tier, deadline, and on-time delivery rate.

HOW TO ACCESS IT

Visit www.fpnaprofessionals.com/precisiontrap to download your free copy or scan the QR code below.

The workbook is updated periodically. Registered users receive access to all future versions automatically.

Take Your Learning Further

This book gives you the argument and the frameworks. The video course gives you the implementation.

The Precision Trap Video Course is a structured online programme designed for finance professionals who want to move from reading about decision-led finance to practising it. It covers every framework in the book in depth, with worked examples, case studies, and practical exercises drawn from real finance situations.

What the course covers:

Decision Tiering in practice. How to apply the three questions across the most common request types your business sends to finance.

The Accuracy Dial. How to calibrate precision to what decisions actually require and how to have that conversation with business partners who expect Tier 3 for everything.

The Stakeholder Contract. How to run the pre-analysis brief conversation in a way that feels natural rather than bureaucratic.

Communication for Action. How to restructure any finance presentation around a decision rather than a report.

The CEO Conversation. How to prepare for and execute the conversation that changes how finance is perceived in your organisation.

The Decision Velocity Scorecard. How to implement the five metrics, present them to your CEO, and use them to drive genuine culture change.

Who it is for: Finance professionals who have read the book and want structured accountability as they implement the ideas. Finance leaders who want to take their team through the frameworks together. Organisations that want to run the programme as a group development initiative.

How to enrol: Visit www.fpnaprofessionals.com/precisiontrap-course or scan the QR Code

References

The following sources informed the ideas, frameworks, and analogies in this book.

BOOKS AND PUBLICATIONS

Fung, Jason. *The Obesity Code: Unlocking the Secrets of Weight Loss.* Greystone Books, 2016.

Fung, Jason. *The Diabetes Code: Prevent and Reverse Type 2 Diabetes Naturally.* Greystone Books, 2018.

Covey, Stephen R. *The 7 Habits of Highly Effective People.* Free Press, 1989.

Muller, Jerry Z. *The Tyranny of Metrics.* Princeton University Press, 2018.

Ohno, Taiichi. *Toyota Production System: Beyond Large-Scale Production.* Productivity Press, 1988.

Kahneman, Daniel. *Thinking, Fast and Slow.* Farrar, Straus and Giroux, 2011.

FRAMEWORKS AND CONCEPTS

Goodhart's Law. Originally articulated by Charles Goodhart in *Monetary Relationships: A View from Threadneedle Street,* 1975.

The McNamara Fallacy. Named after Robert McNamara, United States Secretary of Défense 1961 to 1968. Attributed to sociologist Daniel Yankelovich.

The Streetlight Effect. An observational bias documented across multiple disciplines. Popularised in scientific literature and referenced widely in behavioural economics.

COMMUNITY AND PRACTICE

FP&A Professionals Institute Curriculum. Asif Masani and Dhawal Parvatikar, 2022 to 2026.

CGFPA® Programme Materials. FP&A Professionals Institute, 2023 to 2026.

The real-world stories contributed by Ron Monteiro, Dr. Prashanth Southekal, and Dhawal Parvatikar are drawn from their own professional experience and are used with their explicit permission.

Connect with the Author

Asif Masani writes and speaks about FP&A, decision-led finance, AI in finance, and the evolving role of the modern finance professional.

If this book resonated with you, there are several ways to stay connected and go deeper.

LinkedIn Follow Asif on LinkedIn for daily insights on FP&A, finance leadership, and the ideas behind The Precision Trap. linkedin.com/in/asifmasani

YouTube Subscribe to the @asifmasani channel for video content on FP&A skills, AI in finance, and career development for finance professionals.

FP&A Professionals Institute Explore certifications, courses, and community resources for finance professionals at every stage of their career. www.fpnaprofessionals.com

CGFPA® Certification Learn about the Certified Global FP&A Professional designation and upcoming cohort dates. www.fpnaprofessionals.com/

The Precision Trap Community Join the conversation around the book. Share your story. Tell us where you recognised yourself in these pages. Tell us what changed after you read it. www.fpnaprofessionals.com/precisiontrap

For Speaking and Corporate Training Enquiries If you would like Asif to speak at your event or work with your finance team on escaping the precision trap, reach out directly. info@fpnaprofessionals.com

FP&A Professionals Institute (FPI) Programs

CGFPA®: Certified Global FP&A Professional *Live Cohort Six Month Certification*

The CGFPA® is one of the few globally recognised credentials dedicated exclusively to Financial Planning and Analysis. A six-month, 100+ hour in-depth certification programme covering 10 comprehensive modules including Financial Analysis, Strategy, Financial Modelling, Budgeting and Forecasting, Business Partnering, Data Storytelling, Data Analytics, and AI in Finance.

Technical tools covered include Advanced Excel, Power BI, Tableau, SQL, and Python for finance. AI tools covered include Claude, ChatGPT, Microsoft Copilot, and Google Gemini, as well as agentic AI platforms including Manus.

Designed for finance professionals who want to be recognised globally for their FP&A expertise.

Visit: https://fpnaprofessionals.com/certified-global-fpa-professional-cgfpa/

AIFPA®: AI for Finance Professionals *Live Cohort Certification*

A dedicated certification for finance professionals looking to harness the power of Artificial Intelligence in their day-to-day work. Covers AI tools, prompt engineering for finance, AI-powered forecasting, automation of routine finance tasks, and the future of the finance function in an AI-driven world.

AI tools covered include Claude, ChatGPT, Microsoft Copilot, and Google Gemini, as well as agentic AI platforms including Manus.

Visit: https://fpnaprofessionals.com/ai-for-finance-for-fpa-aifpa/

FPAMC®: FP&A Masterclass *Self-paced*

Learn FP&A with hands-on training in budgeting, forecasting, management reporting, data storytelling, and business partnering. Elevate your FP&A skills to create impact, influence stakeholders, and kickstart your career in FP&A.

Visit: https://fpnaprofessionals.com/fpa-masterclass-fpamc/

FMFPA®: Financial Modelling for FP&A *Self-paced*

The fundamentals of financial modelling built for FP&A professionals. Covers model structure, budgeting, forecasting, scenario analysis, and the practical application of Excel and financial tools in a real business context.

Visit: https://fpnaprofessionals.com/financial-modelling-for-fpa/

FLM: Finance Leadership Masterclass *Self-paced*

A masterclass designed for senior finance professionals ready to step into leadership. Covers the mindset, skills, and behaviours required to lead a finance function that drives decisions rather than documents them. Includes modules on executive communication, stakeholder influence, team culture, and building a decision-led finance function from the inside out.

Visit: https://fpnaprofessionals.com/finance-leadership-masterclass-flm/

The Precision Trap Video Course *Self-paced*

The structured online companion to this book. Covers every framework in depth with worked examples, case studies, and practical exercises. Available for individual enrolment and as a group development programme for finance teams.

Visit: https://fpnaprofessionals.teachable.com/l/pdp/the-precision-trap

For more info and course brochures visit **www.fpnaprofessionals.com**

www.ingramcontent.com/pod-product-compliance
Lightning Source LLC
LaVergne TN
LVHW100309210926
848480LV00003B/1069